John Wesley

Entire Sanctification attainable in this Life

John Wesley
Entire Sanctification attainable in this Life
ISBN/EAN: 9783337178642

Printed in Europe, USA, Canada, Australia, Japan
Cover: Foto ©Lupo / pixelio.de

More available books at **www.hansebooks.com**

ENTIRE SANCTIFICATION

ATTAINABLE IN THIS LIFE

I

Mr. WESLEY'S
PLAIN ACCOUNT OF CHRISTIAN
PERFECTION

II

Mr. FLETCHER'S
PRACTICAL APPLICATION OF
THE DOCTRINE TO VARIOUS CLASSES
OF CHRISTIANS

London:
CHARLES H. KELLY
2, CASTLE STREET, CITY ROAD; AND
26, PATERNOSTER ROW, E.C.
1898

A PLAIN ACCOUNT

OF

CHRISTIAN PERFECTION

BY THE LATE

Rev. JOHN WESLEY, M.A.

A PLAIN ACCOUNT

OF

CHRISTIAN PERFECTION

1. What I purpose in the following pages is, to give a plain and distinct account of the steps by which I was led, during a course of many years, to embrace the doctrine of Christian Perfection. This I owe to the serious part of mankind; those who desire to know all the truth as it is in Jesus. And these only are concerned in questions of this kind. To these I would nakedly declare the thing as it is, endeavouring all along to show, from one period to another, both what I thought, and why I thought so.

2. In the year 1725, being in the twenty-third year of my age, I met with Bishop Taylor's *Rules and Exercises of Holy Living and Dying*. In reading several parts of this book, I was exceedingly affected: that part in particular which relates to purity of intention. Instantly I resolved to dedicate all my

life to God; all my thoughts, and words, and actions; being thoroughly convinced there was no medium, but that every part of my life (not some only) must either be a sacrifice to God, or myself; that is, in effect, to the devil.

Can any serious person doubt of this, or find a medium between serving God, and serving the devil?

3. In the year 1726 I met with Kempis's *Christian's Pattern.* The nature and extent of inward religion, the religion of the heart, now appeared to me in a stronger light than ever it had done before. I saw, that giving even all my life to God (supposing it possible to do this, and go no farther) would profit me nothing, unless I gave my heart, yea all my heart, to Him. I saw that "simplicity of intention, and purity of affection," one design in all we speak or do, and one desire ruling all our tempers, are indeed "the wings of the soul," without which she can never ascend to the mount of God.

4. A year or two after, Mr. Law's *Christian Perfection* and *Serious Call* were put into my hands. These convinced me more than ever of the absolute impossibility of being half a Christian. And I determined, through His grace (the absolute necessity of which I was deeply sensible of), to be all devoted to God,—to give Him all my soul, my body, and my substance.

Will any considerate man say, that this is carrying matters too far? or that anything less is due to Him who has given Himself for us, than to give Him ourselves; all we have, and all we are?

5. In the year 1729 I began not only to read but to study the Bible, as the one, the only standard of truth, and the only model of pure religion. Hence I saw, in a clearer and clearer light, the indispensable necessity of having the mind which was in Christ, and of walking as Christ also walked; even of having not some part only, but all the mind which was in Him; and of walking as He walked, not only in many or in most respects, but in all things. And this was the light wherein, at this time, I generally considered religion, as a uniform following of Christ, an entire inward and outward conformity to our Master. Nor was I afraid of anything more than of bending this rule to the experience of myself, or of other men; of allowing myself in any the least disconformity to our grand Exemplar.

6. On January 1, 1733, I preached before the University, in St. Mary's Church (Oxford), on "the circumcision of the heart"; an account of which I gave in these words: "It is that habitual disposition of soul, which in the sacred writings is termed holiness, and which directly implies the being cleansed from sin; from all filthiness both of flesh and spirit; and, by consequence, the being endued with those virtues which were in Christ Jesus; the being so 'renewed in the image of our mind,' as to be 'perfect as our Father in heaven is perfect'" (*Works*, vol. v. p. 203).

In the same sermon I observed: "'Love is the fulfilling of the law, the end of the commandment.' It is not only the first and great command, but all the commandments in one: 'Whatsoever things are just, whatsoever things are pure, if there be any virtue, if there be any praise,' they are all comprised in this one word, LOVE. In this is perfection, and glory, and happiness! The royal law of heaven and earth is this, 'Thou shalt love the Lord thy God with all thy heart, and with all thy soul, and with all thy mind, and with all thy strength.' The one perfect good shall be your one ultimate end. One thing shall ye desire for its own sake,—the fruition of Him who is all in all. One happiness shall ye propose to your souls, even a union with Him that made them; the having 'fellowship with the Father and the Son'; the being 'joined to the Lord in one spirit.' One design ye are to pursue to the end of time—the enjoyment of God in time and in eternity. Desire other things so far as they tend to this: love the creature, as it leads to the Creator. But in every step you take, be this the glorious point that terminates your view. Let every affection, and thought, and word, and action, be subordinate to this. Whatever ye desire or fear, whatever ye seek or shun, whatever ye think, speak, or do, be it in order to your happiness in God,—the sole end, as well as source, of your being" (*Ibid.*, pp. 207, 208).

I concluded in these words: "Here is

the sum of the perfect law, the circumcision of the heart. Let the spirit return to God that gave it, with the whole train of its affections. Other sacrifices from us He would not: but the living sacrifice of the heart hath He chosen. Let it be continually offered up to God, through Christ, in flames of holy love. And let no creature be suffered to share with Him; for He is a jealous God. His throne will He not divide with another; He will reign without a rival. Be no design, no desire, admitted there, but what has Him for its ultimate object. This is the way wherein those children of God once walked, who being dead, still speak to us. Desire not to live but to praise His name; let all your thoughts, words, and works tend to His glory. Let your soul be filled with so entire a love to Him, that you may love nothing but for His sake. Have a pure intention of heart, a steadfast regard to His glory in all your actions. For then, and not till then, is that mind in us which was also in Christ Jesus, when in every motion of our heart, in every word of our tongue, in every work of our hands, we pursue nothing but in relation to Him, and in subordination to His pleasure; when we, too, neither think, nor speak, nor act, to fulfil our own will, but the will of Him that sent us; when 'whether we eat or drink, or whatever we do, we do it all to the glory of God'" (*Ibid.*, p. 211).

It may be observed, this sermon was composed the first of all my writings which have been published. This was the view of religion I then had, which even then I scrupled not to term Perfection. This is the view I have of it now, without any material addition or diminution. And what is there here which any man of understanding, who believes the Bible, can object to? What can he deny, without flatly contradicting the Scripture? what retrench, without taking from the word of God?

7. In the same sentiment did my brother and I remain (with all those young gentlemen in derision termed Methodists) till we embarked for America, in the latter end of 1735. It was the next year, while I was at Savannah, that I wrote the following lines:—

"Is there a thing beneath the sun
  That strives with Thee my heart to share?
Ah, tear it thence, and reign alone,
  The Lord of every motion there!"

In the beginning of the year 1738, as I was returning from thence, the cry of my heart was—

"O grant that nothing in my soul
  May dwell, but Thy pure love alone!
O may Thy love possess me whole,
  My joy, my treasure, and my crown;
Strange fires far from my heart remove;
My every act, word, thought, be love!"

I never heard that any one objected to this. And indeed who can object? Is not this the language not only of every believer, but of every one that is truly awakened? But what have I written to this day, which is either stronger or plainer?

8. In August following, I had a long conversation with Arvid Gradin, in Germany. After he had given me an account of his experience, I desired him to give me, in writing, a definition of "the full assurance of faith," which he did in the following words:—

"*Requies in sanguine Christi; firma fiducia in Deum, et persuasio de gratia divina; tranquillitas mentis summa, atque serenitas et pax; cum absentia omnis desiderii carnalis, et cessatione peccatorum etiam internorum.*"

"Repose in the blood of Christ; a firm confidence in God, and persuasion of His favour; the highest tranquillity, serenity, and peace of mind; with a deliverance from every fleshly desire, and a cessation of all, even inward sins."

This was the first account I ever heard from any living man of what I had before learned myself from the oracles of God, and had been praying for (with the little company of my friends), and expecting for several years.

9. In 1739 my brother and I published a volume of *Hymns and Sacred Poems*. In many of these we declared our sentiments strongly and explicitly. So, page 24—

"Turn the full stream of nature's tide !
   Let all our actions tend
To Thee, their source : Thy love the guide,
   Thy glory be the end.

> Earth then a scale to heaven shall be;
>   Sense shall point out the road;
> The creatures all shall lead to Thee,
>   And all we taste be God."

Again:

> "Lord, arm me with Thy Spirit's might,
>   Since I am call'd by Thy great name;
> In Thee my wandering thoughts unite,
>   Of all my works be Thou the aim:
> Thy love attend me all my days,
> And my sole business be Thy praise." (P. 122.)

Again:

> "Eager for Thee I ask and pant;
>   So strong the principle Divine,
> Carries me out with sweet constraint,
>   Till all my hallow'd soul be Thine;
> Plunged in the Godhead's deepest sea,
> And lost in Thine immensity!" (P. 125.)

Once more:

> "Heavenly Adam, life Divine,
> Change my nature into Thine;
> Move and spread throughout my soul,
> Actuate and fill the whole." (P. 153.)

It would be easy to cite many more passages to the same effect. But these are sufficient to show, beyond contradiction, what our sentiments then were.

10. The first tract I ever wrote expressly on this subject, was published in the latter end of this year. That none might be prejudiced before they read it, I gave it the indifferent title of *The Character of a Methodist*. In this I described a perfect Christian; placing in the front, "Not as though I had already attained." Part of it I subjoin without any alteration :—

"A Methodist is one who loves the Lord his God with all his heart, with all his soul, with all his mind, and with all his strength. God is the joy of his heart, and the desire of his soul, which is continually crying, 'Whom have I in heaven but Thee? and there is none upon earth whom I desire besides Thee.' My God and my all! 'Thou art the strength of my heart, and my portion for ever.' He is therefore happy in God; yea, always happy; as having in Him a well of water springing up into everlasting life, and overflowing his soul with peace and joy. Perfect love having now cast out fear, he rejoices evermore. Yea, his joy is full; and all his bones cry out, 'Blessed be the God and Father of our Lord Jesus Christ, who, according to His abundant mercy, hath begotten me again unto a living hope of an inheritance incorruptible and undefiled, reserved in heaven for me.'

"And he who hath this hope, thus full of immortality, 'in everything giveth thanks'; as knowing this (whatsoever it is) is the will of God in Christ Jesus concerning him. From Him, therefore, he cheerfully receives all, saying, 'Good is the will of the Lord'; and whether He giveth or taketh away, equally blessing the Name of the Lord. Whether in ease or pain, whether in sickness or health, whether in life or death, he giveth thanks from the ground of the heart to Him who orders it for good; into whose hands he hath wholly committed his body and soul, 'as into the hands of a faithful Creator.'

He is therefore anxiously 'careful for nothing,' as having 'cast all his care on Him that careth for him'; and 'in all things' resting on Him, after 'making his request known to Him with thanksgiving.'

"For indeed he 'prays without ceasing': at all times the language of his heart is this: 'Unto Thee is my mouth, though without a voice; and my silence speaketh unto Thee.' His heart is lifted up to God at all times, and in all places. In this he is never hindered, much less interrupted, by any person or thing. In retirement or company, in leisure, business, or conversation, his heart is ever with the Lord. Whether he lie down or rise up, God is in all his thoughts: he walks with God continually; having the loving eye of his soul fixed on Him, and everywhere 'seeing Him that is invisible.'

"And loving God, he 'loves his neighbour as himself'; he loves every man as his own soul. He loves his enemies; yea, and the enemies of God. And if it be not in his power to 'do good to them that hate him,' yet he ceases not to 'pray for them,' though they spurn his love, and still 'despitefully use him, and persecute him.'

"For he 'is pure in heart.' Love has purified his heart from envy, malice, wrath, and every unkind temper. It has cleansed him from pride, whereof only 'cometh contention': and he hath now 'put on bowels of mercies, kindness, humbleness of mind, meekness, long-suffering.' And, indeed, all possible ground for contention on his part is cut off. For none can take from him what he desires, seeing he 'loves not the world, nor any of the things of the world'; but 'all his desire is unto God, and to the remembrance of His Name.'

"Agreeable to this, his one desire is the one design of his life, namely, 'to do not his own will, but the will of Him that sent him.' His one intention at all times and in all places is, not to please Himself, but Him whom his soul loveth. He hath a single eye; and because his 'eye is single, his whole body is full of light.' The whole is light, as when 'the bright shining of a candle doth enlighten the house.' God reigns alone: all that is in the soul is holiness to the Lord. There is not a motion in his heart but is according to His will. Every thought that arises points to Him, and is in obedience to the law of Christ.

"And the tree is known by its fruits. For as he loves God, 'so he keeps His commandments': not only some, or most of them, but ALL, from the least to the greatest. He is not content to 'keep the whole law, and offend in one point,' but has, in all points, 'a conscience void of offence, towards God, and towards man.' Whatever God has forbidden, he avoids; whatever God has enjoined, he does. 'He runs the way of God's commandments,' now He hath set his heart at liberty. It is his glory and joy so to do: it is his daily crown of rejoicing, to do the will of God on earth as it is done in heaven.

"All the commandments of God he

accordingly keeps, and that with all his might. For his obedience is in proportion to His love, the source from whence it flows. And therefore loving God with all his heart, he serves Him with all his strength. He continually presents his soul and body a 'living sacrifice, holy, acceptable to God'; entirely and without reserve, devoting himself, all he has, all he is, to His glory. All the talents he has, he constantly employs according to his Master's will; every power and faculty of his soul, every member of his body.

"By consequence, 'whatsoever he doeth, it is all to the glory of God.' In all his employments of every kind, he not only aims at this (which is implied in having a single eye), but actually attains it. His business and his refreshments, as well as his prayers, all serve to this great end. Whether he 'sit in the house, or walk by the way,' whether he lie down, or rise up, he is promoting, in all he speaks, or does, the one business of his life. Whether he put on his apparel, or labour, or eat and drink, or divert himself from too wasting labour, it all tends to advance the glory of God, by peace and good-will among men. His one invariable rule is this: 'Whatsoever ye do in word or deed, do it all in the name of the Lord Jesus, giving thanks to God, even the Father, through Him.'

"Nor do the customs of the world at all hinder his 'running the race which is set before him.' He cannot, therefore, 'lay up treasures upon earth,' no more than he can take fire into his bosom. He cannot speak evil of his neighbour, any more than he can lie either to God or man. He cannot utter an unkind word of anyone; for love keeps the door of his lips. He cannot speak idle words; no corrupt conversation ever comes out of his mouth; as is all that is not good to the use of edifying, not fit to minister grace to the hearers. But 'whatsoever things are pure, whatsoever things are lovely, whatsoever things are' justly 'of good report,' he thinks, speaks, and acts, 'adorning the doctrine of God our Saviour in all things.'"

These are the very words wherein I largely declared, for the first time, my sentiments of Christian Perfection. And is it not easy to see—(1) That this is the very point at which I aimed all along from the year 1725; and more determinately from the gear 1730, when I began to be *homo unius libri,* "a man of one book," regarding none, comparatively, but the Bible? Is it not easy to see—(2) That this is the very same doctrine which I believe and teach at this day; not adding one point, either to that inward or outward holiness which I maintained eight-and-thirty years ago? And it is the same which, by the grace of God, I have continued to teach from that time till now; as will appear to every impartial person from the extracts subjoined below.

11. I do not know that any writer has made any objection against that tract to this day. And for some time I did not find much opposition upon that head; at least, not from serious persons. But after

a time a cry arose, and (what a little surprised me) among religious men, who affirmed, not that I stated perfection wrong, but that "there is no perfection on earth"; nay, and fell vehemently on my brother and me for affirming the contrary. We scarce expected so rough an attack from these; especially as we were clear on justification by faith, and careful to ascribe the whole of salvation to the mere grace of God. But what most surprised us was, that we were said to "dishonour Christ," by asserting that He "saveth to the uttermost"; by maintaining He will reign in our hearts alone, and subdue all things to Himself.

12. I think it was in the latter end of the year 1740 that I had a conversation with Dr. Gibson, then Bishop of London, at Whitehall. He asked me what I meant by Perfection. I told him without any disguise or reserve. When I ceased speaking he said, "Mr. Wesley, if this be all you mean, publish it to all the world. If any one then can confute what you say, he may have free leave." I answered, "My Lord, I will"; and accordingly wrote and published the sermon on Christian Perfection.

In this I endeavoured to show—(1) In what sense Christians are not, (2) in what sense they are, perfect.

"1. In what sense they are not. They are not perfect in knowledge. They are not free from ignorance; no, nor from mistake. We are no more to expect any living man to be infallible, than to be omniscient. They are not free from infirmities, such as weakness or slowness of understanding, irregular quickness or heaviness of imagination. Such, in another kind, are, impropriety of language, ungracefulness of pronunciation; to which one might add a thousand nameless defects, either in conversation or behaviour. From such infirmities as these none are perfectly freed till their spirits return to God. Neither can we expect, till then, to be wholly freed from temptation: 'for the servant is not above his Master.' But neither in this sense is there any absolute perfection on earth. There is no perfection of degrees; none which does not admit of a continual increase.

"2. In what sense, then, are they perfect? Observe, we are not now speaking of babes in Christ, but adult Christians. But even babes in Christ are so far perfect as not to commit sin. This St. John affirms expressly; and it cannot be disproved by the examples of the Old Testament. For what if the holiest of the ancient Jews did sometimes commit sin? We cannot infer from hence, that 'all Christians do and must commit sin as long as they live.'

"But does not the Scripture say, 'A just man sinneth seven times a day?' It does not. Indeed it says, 'A just man falleth seven times.' But this is quite another thing. For, first, the words, *a day*, are not in the text. Secondly, here is no mention of falling into sin at all. What is here mentioned is falling into temporal affliction.

"But elsewhere Solomon says, 'There is no man that sinneth not.' Doubtless thus it was in the days of Solomon; yea, and from Solomon to Christ there was then no man that sinned not. But whatever was the case of those under the law, we may safely affirm, with St. John, that since the Gospel was given, 'he that is born of God sinneth not.'

"The privileges of Christians are in no wise to be measured by what the Old Testament records concerning those who were under the Jewish dispensation; seeing the fulness of time is now come; the Holy Ghost is now given; the great salvation of God is now brought to men by the revelation of Jesus Christ. The kingdom of heaven is now set up on earth, concerning which the Spirit of God declared of old time (so far is David from being the pattern or standard of Christian perfection), 'He that is feeble among them at that day shall be as David; and the house of David shall be as the angel of the Lord before them' (Zech. xii. 8).

"But the apostles themselves committed sin: Peter by dissembling, Paul by his sharp contention with Barnabas. Suppose they did, will you argue thus: 'If two of the apostles once committed sin, then all other Christians, in all ages, do and must commit sin as long as they live?' Nay, God forbid we should thus speak. No necessity of sin was laid upon them: the grace of God was surely sufficient for them; and it is sufficient for us at this day.

"But St. James says, 'In many things we offend all.' True: but who are the persons here spoken of? Why, those *many masters* or teachers whom God had not sent. Not the apostle himself, nor any real Christian. That in the word *we* (used by a figure of speech, common in all other as well as the inspired writings) the apostle could not possibly include himself, or any other true believer, appears, first, from the ninth verse: 'Therewith bless *we* God, and therewith curse *we* men.' Surely not *we apostles!* not *we believers!* Secondly, from the words preceding the text: 'My brethren, be not many masters,' or teachers, 'knowing that we shall receive the greater condemnation: for in many things we offend all.' *We!* Who? Not the apostles, nor true believers, but they who were to 'receive the greater condemnation,' because of those many offences. Nay, thirdly, the verse itself proves, that '*we offend all*' cannot be spoken either of all men, or all Christians. For in it immediately follows the mention of a man *who offends not*, as the *we* first mentioned did; from whom, therefore, he is professedly contra-distinguished, and pronounced a *perfect man*.

"But St. John himself says, 'If we say that we have no sin, we deceive ourselves'; and, 'if we say we have not sinned, we make Him a liar, and His word is not in us.'

"I answer—(1) The tenth verse fixes the sense of the eighth. 'If we say we have no sin,' in the former, being explained by, 'If we say we have not sinned,' in the latter verse. (2) The point of consideration is not whether we have or have not sinned heretofore; and neither of these verses asserts that we do sin, or commit sin now. (3) The ninth verse explains both the eighth and tenth: 'If we confess our sins, He is faithful and just to forgive us our sins, and to cleanse us from all unrighteousness.' As if we had said, I have before affirmed, 'The blood of Christ cleanseth from all sin.' And no man can say, 'I need it not; I have no sin to be cleansed from.' 'If we say we have no sin,' that we have not sinned, 'we deceive ourselves,' and make God a liar. But 'if we confess our sins, He is faithful and just,' not only 'to forgive us our sins, but also to cleanse us from all unrighteousness,' that we may 'go and sin no more.' In conformity, therefore, both to the doctrine of St. John, and the whole tenor of the New Testament, we fix this conclusion: A Christian is so far perfect as not to commit sin.

"This is the glorious privilege of every Christian, yea, though he be but a babe in Christ. But it is only of grown Christians it can be affirmed they are in such a sense perfect, as, secondly, to be freed from evil thoughts and evil tempers. First, from evil or sinful thoughts. Indeed, whence should they spring? 'Out of the heart of man,' if at all, 'proceed evil thoughts.' If, therefore, the heart be no longer evil, then evil thoughts no longer proceed out of it. For, 'a good tree cannot bring forth evil fruit.'

"And as they are freed from evil

thoughts, so likewise from evil tempers. Every one of these can say, with St. Paul, 'I am crucified with Christ: nevertheless I live; yet not I, but Christ liveth in me'; words that manifestly describe a deliverance from inward as well as from outward sin. This is expressed both negatively, 'I live not,'—my evil nature, the body of sin, is destroyed; and positively, 'Christ liveth in me,'—and, therefore, all that is holy and just and good. Indeed, both these, 'Christ liveth in me,' and 'I live not,' are inseparably connected. For what communion hath light with darkness, or Christ with Belial?

"He, therefore, who liveth in these Christians, hath purified their hearts by faith; insomuch that every one that has Christ in him, 'the hope of glory, purifieth himself even as He is pure.' He is purified from pride; for Christ was lowly in heart. He is pure from desire and self-will: for Christ desired only to do the will of His Father. And He is pure from anger, in the common sense of the word; for Christ was meek and gentle. I say, in the common sense of the word; for He is angry at sin while He is grieved for the sinner. He feels a displacency at every offence against God, but only tender compassion to the offender.

"Thus doth Jesus save His people from their sins; not only from outward sins, but from the sins of their hearts. 'True,' say some, 'but not till death; not in this world.' Nay, St. John says, 'Herein is our love made perfect, that we may have boldness in the day of judgment;

because, as He is, so are we in this world.' The apostle here, beyond all contradiction, speaks of himself and other living Christians, of whom he flatly affirms, that not only at or after death, but 'in this world,' they are as their Master.

"Exactly agreeable to this are his words in the first chapter: 'God is light, and in Him is no darkness at all. If we walk in the light, as He is in the light, we have fellowship one with another, and the blood of Jesus Christ His Son cleanseth us from all sin.' And again: 'If we confess our sins, He is faithful and just to forgive us our sins, and to cleanse us from all unrighteousness.' Now, it is evident the apostle here speaks of a deliverance wrought in this world. For he saith not, The blood of Christ *will* cleanse (at the hour of death, or in the day of judgment), but it 'cleanseth,' at the present time, us living Christians 'from all sin.' And it is equally evident, that if any sin remain, we are not cleansed from all sin. If *any* unrighteousness remain in the soul, it is not cleansed from all unrighteousness. Neither let any say that this relates to justification only, or the cleansing us from the guilt of sin— First, because this is confounding together what the apostle clearly distinguishes; who mentions first, 'to forgive us our sins,' and then, 'to cleanse us from all unrighteousness.' Secondly, because this is asserting justification by works in the strongest sense possible. It is making all inward, as well as all outward holiness, necessarily previous to justification. For if the cleansing here spoken of is no other than the cleansing us from the guilt of sin, then we are not cleansed from guilt, that is, not justified, unless on condition of walking 'in the light as He is in the light.' It remains, then, that Christians are saved in this world from all sin, from all unrighteousness; that they are now in such a sense perfect, as not to commit sin, and to be freed from evil thoughts and evil tempers."

It could not be but that a discourse of this kind, which directly contradicted the favourite opinion of many, who were esteemed by others, and possibly esteemed themselves, some of the best Christians (whereas, if these things were so, they were not Christians at all), should give no small offence. Many answers or animadversions, therefore, were expected; but I was agreeably disappointed. I do not know that any appeared : so I went quietly on my way.

13. Not long after, I think in the spring, 1741, we published a second volume of hymns. As the doctrine was still much misunderstood, and consequently misrepresented, I judged it needful to explain yet farther upon the head; which was done in the preface to it as follows :—

"This great gift of God, the salvation of our souls, is no other than the image of God fresh stamped on our hearts. It is a 'renewal of believers in the spirit of their minds, after the likeness of Him that created them.' God hath now laid 'the axe unto the root of the tree,' 'purifying their hearts by faith,' and 'cleansing all the thoughts of their hearts by the inspiration of His Holy Spirit.' Having this hope that they shall see God as He is, they 'purify themselves even as He is pure'; and are 'holy, as He that hath called them is holy, in all manner of conversation.' Not that they have already attained all that they shall attain, either are already (in this sense) perfect. But they daily 'go on from strength to strength'; 'beholding' now, 'as in a glass, the glory of the Lord, they are changed into the same image, from glory to glory, by the Spirit of the Lord.'

"And 'where the Spirit of the Lord is, there is liberty'; such liberty 'from the law of sin and death' as the children of this world will not believe, though a man declare it unto them. 'The Son hath made them free,' who are thus 'born of God,' from that great root of sin and bitterness, pride. They feel that all their 'sufficiency is of God'; that it is He alone who 'is in all their thoughts,' and 'worketh in them both to will and to do of His good pleasure.' They feel that 'it is not they' that 'speak, but the Spirit of' their 'Father who speaketh in them'; and that whatsoever is done by their hands, 'the Father, who is in them, He doeth the works.' So that God is to them all in all, and they are nothing in His sight. They are freed from self-will, as desiring nothing but the holy and perfect will of God: not supplies in want, not ease in pain,[1] nor life, or

---

[1] This is too strong. Our Lord Himself desired ease in pain. He asked for it, only with

death, or any creature; but continually crying in their inmost soul, 'Father, Thy will be done.' They are freed from evil thoughts, so that they cannot enter into them; no, not for a moment. Aforetime, when an evil thought came in, they looked up, and it vanished away. But now it does not come in, there being no room for this in a soul which is full of God. They are free from wanderings in prayer. Whensoever they pour out their hearts in a more immediate manner before God, they have no thought [1] of anything past, or absent, or to come, but of God alone. In times past they had wandering thoughts darted in, which yet fled away like smoke; but now that smoke does not rise at all. They have no fear or doubt, either as to their state in general, or as to any particular action.[2] The 'unction from the Holy One' teacheth them every hour what they shall do, and what they shall speak.[3] Nor, therefore, have they any need to reason concerning it.[4] They are, in one sense, freed from temptation: for though numberless temptations fly about them, yet they trouble them not.[5] At all times their resignation: *Not as I will*, I desire, *but as Thou wilt*.

[1] This is far too strong. See the Sermon on *Wandering Thoughts*.

[2] Frequently this is the case, but only *for a time*.

[3] For a time it may be so; but not always.

[4] Sometimes they have no need; at other times they have.

[5] Sometimes they do not; at other times they do, and that grievously.

souls are even and calm, their hearts are steadfast and unmovable. Their peace, flowing as a river, 'passeth all understanding,' and they 'rejoice with joy unspeakable and full of glory.' For 'they are sealed by the Spirit unto the day of redemption'; having the witness in themselves, that 'there is laid up for them a crown of righteousness, which the Lord will give' them 'in that day.'[1]

"Not that every one is a child of the devil till he is thus renewed in love. On the contrary, whoever has a sure 'confidence in God, that, through the merits of Christ his sins are forgiven,' he is a child of God, and, if he abide in Him, an heir of all the promises. Neither ought he in any wise to cast away his confidence, or to deny the faith he has received, because it is weak, or because it is 'tried with fire,' so that his soul is 'in heaviness through manifold temptations.'

"Neither dare we affirm, as some have done, that all this salvation is given at once. There is indeed an instantaneous, as well as a gradual, work of God in His children; and there wants not, we know, a cloud of witnesses who have received, in one moment, either a clear sense of the forgiveness of their sins, or the abiding witness of the Holy Spirit. But we do not know a single instance, in any place, of a person's receiving, in one and the same moment, remission of sins, the abid-

---

[1] Not all who are saved from sin; many of them have not attained it yet.

ing witness of the Spirit, and a new, a clean heart.

"Indeed, how God may work, we cannot tell; but the general manner wherein He does work is this: Those who once trusted in themselves that they were righteous, that they were rich, and increased in goods, and had need of nothing, are, by the Spirit of God applying His word, convinced that they are poor and naked. All the things that they have done are brought to their remembrance, and set in array before them; so that they see the wrath of God hanging over their heads, and feel that they deserve the damnation of hell. In their trouble they cry unto the Lord, and He shows them that He hath taken away their sins, and opens the kingdom of heaven in their hearts, 'righteousness, and peace, and joy in the Holy Ghost.' Sorrow and pain are fled away, and sin has no more dominion over them. Knowing they are justified freely, through faith in His blood, they 'have peace with God through Jesus Christ'; they 'rejoice in hope of the glory of God,' and 'the love of God is shed abroad in their hearts.'

"In this peace they remain for days, or weeks, or months, and commonly suppose that they shall not know war any more; till some of their old enemies, their bosom sins, or the sin which did most easily beset them (perhaps anger or desire), assault them again, and thrust sore at them that they may fall. Then arises fear that they should not endure to the end; and often doubt whether God has not forgotten them, or whether they did not deceive themselves in thinking their sins were forgiven. Under these clouds, especially if they reason with the devil, they go mourning all the day long. But it is seldom long before their Lord answers for Himself, sending them the Holy Ghost to comfort them, to bear witness continually with their spirits that they are the children of God. Then they are indeed meek, and gentle, and teachable, even as a little child. And now first do they see the ground of their heart,[1] which God before would not disclose unto them, lest the soul should fail before Him, and the spirit which He had made. Now they see all the hidden abominations there, the depths of pride, self-will, and hell; yet having the witness in themselves, 'Thou art an heir of God, a joint-heir with Christ,' even in the midst of this fiery trial; which continually heightens both the strong sense they then have of their inability to help themselves, and the inexpressible hunger they feel after a full renewal in His image, in 'righteousness and true holiness.' Then God is mindful of the desire of them that fear Him, and gives them a single eye and a pure heart; He stamps upon them His own image and superscription; He createth

---

[1] Is it not astonishing that, while this book is extant, which was published four-and-twenty years ago, any one should face me down that this is a new doctrine, and what I never taught before? [This note was first published in the year 1765.—EDIT.]

them anew in Christ Jesus; He cometh unto them with His Son and blessed Spirit; and, fixing His abode in their souls, bringeth them into the 'rest which remaineth for the people of God.'"

Here I cannot but remark—(1) That this is the strongest account we ever gave of Christian perfection; indeed, too strong in more than one particular, as is observed in the notes annexed; (2) that there is nothing which we have since advanced upon the subject, either in verse or prose, which is not either directly or indirectly contained in this preface. So that, whether our present doctrine be right or wrong, it is, however, the same which we taught from the beginning.

14. I need not give additional proofs of this, by multiplying quotations from the volume itself. It may suffice to cite part of one hymn only, the last in that volume:—

> "Lord, I believe a rest remains
>   To all Thy people known;
> A rest where pure enjoyment reigns,
>   And Thou art loved alone.
>
> A rest where all our soul's desire
>   Is fixed on things above;
> Where doubt, and pain, and fear expire,
>   Cast out by perfect love.
>
> From every evil motion freed
>   (The Son hath made us free),
> On all the powers of hell we tread,
>   In glorious liberty.
>
> Safe in the way of life, above
>   Death, earth, and hell we rise;
> We find, when perfected in love,
>   Our long-sought paradise.

O that I now the rest might know,
  Believe, and enter in!
Now, Saviour, now the power bestow,
  And let me cease from sin!

Remove this hardness from my heart,
  This unbelief remove;
To me the rest of faith impart,
  The Sabbath of Thy love.

Come, O my Saviour, come away!
  Into my soul descend;
No longer from thy creature stay,
  My Author and my End.

The bliss Thou hast for me prepared
  No longer be delay'd;
Come, my exceeding great reward,
  For whom I first was made.

Come, Father, Son, and Holy Ghost,
  And seal me Thine abode!
Let all I am in Thee be lost;
  Let all be lost in God."

Can anything be more clear than—(1) That here also is as full and high a salvation as we have ever spoken of? (2) That this is spoken of as receivable by mere faith, and as hindered only by unbelief? (3) That this faith, and consequently the salvation which it brings, is spoken of as given in an instant? (4) That it is supposed that instant may be now; that we need not stay another moment; that "now," the very "now, is the accepted time; now is the day of" this full "salvation"? And, lastly, that if any speak otherwise, he is the person that brings new doctrine among us?

15. About a year after, namely, in the

year 1742, we published another volume of hymns. The dispute being now at the height, we spoke upon the head more largely than ever before. Accordingly, abundance of the hymns in this volume treat expressly on this subject. And so does the preface, which, as it is short, it may not be amiss to insert entire:—

"(1) Perhaps the general prejudice against Christian perfection may chiefly arise from a misapprehension of the nature of it. We willingly allow, and continually declare, there is no such perfection in this life as implies either a dispensation from doing good, and attending all the ordinances of God; or a freedom from ignorance, mistake, temptation, and a thousand infirmities necessarily connected with flesh and blood.

"(2) First, we not only allow, but earnestly contend, that there is no perfection in this life which implies any dispensation from attending all the ordinances of God; or from doing good unto all men while we have time, though 'especially unto the household of faith.' We believe that not only the babes in Christ, who have newly found redemption in His blood, but those also who are 'grown up into perfect men,' are indispensably obliged, as often as they have opportunity, to 'eat bread and drink wine in remembrance of Him,' and to 'search the Scriptures,' by fasting, as well as temperance, 'to keep their bodies under, and bring them into subjection'; and, above all, to pour out their souls in prayer, both secretly, and in the great congregation.

"(3) We, secondly, believe that there is no such perfection in this life as implies an entire deliverance, either from ignorance or mistake, in things not essential to salvation, or from manifold temptations, or from numberless infirmities, wherewith the corruptible body more or less presses down the soul. We cannot find any ground in Scripture to suppose that any inhabitant of a house of clay is wholly exempt either from bodily infirmities, or from ignorance of many things; or to imagine any is incapable of mistake, or falling into divers temptations.

"(4) But whom then do you mean by 'one that is *perfect*?' We mean one in 'whom is the mind which was in Christ,' and who so 'walketh as Christ also walked'; a man 'that hath clean hands and a pure heart,' or that is 'cleansed from all filthiness of flesh and spirit': one in whom is 'no occasion of stumbling,' and who accordingly 'does not commit sin.' To declare this a little more particularly: We understand by that scriptural expression, 'a perfect man,' one in whom God hath fulfilled His faithful word, 'From all your filthiness and from all your idols I will cleanse you: I will also save you from all your uncleannesses.' We understand hereby, one whom God hath 'sanctified throughout, in body, soul, and spirit'; one who 'walketh in the light as He is in the light; in whom is no darkness at all: the blood of Jesus

Christ His Son having cleansed him from all sin.'

"(5) This man can now testify to all mankind, 'I am crucified with Christ: nevertheless I live; yet not I, but Christ liveth in me.' He is 'holy as God who called him is holy,' both in heart and 'in all manner of conversation.' He 'loveth the Lord his God with all his heart,' and serveth Him with 'all his strength.' He 'loveth his neighbour,' every man, 'as himself'; 'yea,' as Christ 'loveth us'; them in particular that 'despitefully use him, and persecute him, because they know not the Son, neither the Father.' Indeed his soul is all love; filled with 'bowels of mercies, kindness, meekness, gentleness, long-suffering.' And his life agreeth thereto, full of 'the work of faith, the patience of hope, the labour of love.' 'And whatsoever he doeth, either in word or deed, he doeth it all in the name,' in the love and power, 'of the Lord Jesus.' In a word, he doeth 'the will of God on earth, as it is done in heaven.'

"(6) This it is to be a perfect man, to be 'sanctified throughout'; even 'to have a heart so all-flaming with the love of God' (to use Archbishop Usher's word), 'as continually to offer up every thought, word, and work, as a spiritual sacrifice, acceptable to God, through Christ'; in every thought of our hearts, in every word of our tongues, in every work of our hands, to 'show forth His praise, who hath called us out of darkness into His marvellous light.' Oh that both we, and all who seek the Lord Jesus in sincerity, may thus be made perfect in one!"

This is the doctrine which we preached from the beginning, and which we preach at this day. Indeed, by viewing it in every point of light, and comparing it again and again with the word of God on the one hand, and the experience of the children of God on the other, we saw farther into the nature and properties of Christian perfection. But still there is no contrariety at all between our first and our last sentiments. Our first conception of it was, It is to have "the mind which was in Christ," and to "walk as He walked"; to have all the mind that was in Him, and always to walk as He walked: in other words, to be inwardly and outwardly devoted to God; all devoted in heart and life. And we have the same conception of it now, without either addition or diminution.

16. The hymns concerning it in this volume are too numerous to transcribe. I shall only cite a part of three:—

" Saviour from sin, I wait to prove
    That Jesus is Thy healing name;
To lose, when perfected in love,
    Whate'er I have, or can, or am:
I stay me on Thy faithful word,
'The servant shall be as his Lord.'

Answer that gracious end in me
    For which Thy precious life was given;
Redeem from all iniquity,
    Restore, and make me meet for heaven.
Unless Thou purge my every stain,
Thy suffering and my faith are vain.

Didst Thou not die, that I might live
  No longer to myself, but Thee ?
Might body, soul, and spirit give
  To Him who gave Himself for me ?
Come then, my Master, and my God,
Take the dear purchase of Thy blood.

Thy own peculiar servant claim,
  For Thy own truth and mercy's sake ;
Hallow in me Thy glorious name ;
  Me for Thine own this moment take,
And change and throughly purify ;
Thine only may I live and die."   (P. 80.)

"Choose from the world, if now I stand,
  Adorn'd with righteousness divine ;
If, brought into the promised land,
  I justly call the Saviour mine ;
The sanctifying Spirit pour,
  To quench my thirst, and wash me clean ;
Now, Saviour, let the gracious shower
  Descend, and make me pure from sin.

Purge me from every sinful blot ;
  My idols all be cast aside :
Cleanse me from every evil thought,
  From all the filth of self and pride.
The hatred of the carnal mind
  Out of my flesh at once remove :
Give me a tender heart, resigned,
  And pure, and full of faith and love.

Oh that I now, from sin released,
  Thy word might to the utmost prove,
Enter into Thy promised rest,
  The Canaan of Thy perfect love.
Now let me gain perfection's height !
  Now let me into nothing fall,
Be less than nothing in my sight,
  And feel that Christ is all in all ! " (P. 258.)

" Lord, I believe Thy work of grace
  Is perfect in the soul !
His heart is pure who sees Thy face,
  His spirit is made whole.

> From every sickness, by Thy word,
>   From every foul disease,
> Saved, and to perfect health restored,
>   To perfect holiness.
>
> He walks in glorious liberty,
>   To sin entirely dead;
> The Truth, the Son, hath made him free,
>   And he is free indeed.
>
> Throughout his soul Thy glories shine,
>   His soul is all renew'd,
> And deck'd in righteousness divine,
>   And clothed and fill'd with God.
>
> This is the rest, the life, the peace,
>   Which all Thy people prove;
> Love is the bond of perfectness,
>   And all their soul is love.
>
> O joyful sound of Gospel grace;
>   Christ shall in me appear;
> I, even I, shall see His face,
>   I shall be holy here.
>
> He visits now the house of clay,
>   He shakes His future home;
> O wouldst Thou, Lord, on this glad day,
>   Into Thy temple come.
>
> Come, O my God, Thyself reveal,
>   Fill all this mighty void;
> Thou only canst my spirit fill;
>   Come, O my God, my God!
>
> Fulfil, fulfil my large desires,
>   Large as infinity;
> Give, give me all my soul requires,
>   All, all that is in Thee." (P. 298.)

17. On Monday, June 25, 1744, our first conference began, six clergymen and all our preachers being present. The next morning we seriously considered the doctrine of sanctification, or perfection.

The questions asked concerning it, and the substance of the answers given, were as follows:—

" Q. What is it to be *sanctified*?

" A. To be renewed in the image of God, *in righteousness and true holiness.*

" Q. What is implied in being a *perfect Christian*?

" A. The loving God with all our heart, and mind, and soul (Deut. vi. 5).

" Q. Does this imply that *all inward sin* is taken away?

" A. Undoubtedly: or how can we be said to be *saved from all our uncleanness*?" (Ezek. xxxvi. 29).

Our second conference began August 1, 1745. The next morning we spoke of sanctification as follows:—

" Q. When does inward sanctification begin?

" A. In the moment a man is justified. (Yet sin remains in him; yea, the seed of all sin, till he is *sanctified throughout.*) From that time a believer gradually dies to sin, and grows in grace.

" Q. Is this ordinarily given till a little before death?

" A. It is not, to those who expect it no sooner.

" Q. But may we expect it sooner?

" A. Why not? For although we grant—(1) That the generality of believers, whom we have hitherto known, were not so sanctified till near death; (2) that few of those to whom St. Paul wrote his Epistles were so at that time; nor (3) he himself at the time of writing his former

Epistles; yet all this does not prove that we may not be so *to-day*.

"Q. In what manner should we preach sanctification?

"A. Scarce at all to those who are not pressing forward: to those who are, always by way of promise; always *drawing* rather than *driving*."

Our third conference began Tuesday, May 26, 1746.

In this we carefully read over the minutes of the two preceding conferences, to observe whether anything contained therein might be retrenched or altered, on more mature consideration. But we did not see cause to alter in any respect what we had agreed upon before.

Our fourth conference began on Tuesday, June the 16th, 1747. As several persons were present who did not believe the doctrine of perfection, we agreed to examine it from the foundation.

In order to this, it was asked—

"How much is allowed by our brethren who differ from us with regard to entire sanctification?

"A. They grant—(1) That every one must be entirely sanctified in the article of death; (2) that, till then, a believer daily grows in grace, comes nearer and nearer to perfection; (3) that we ought to be continually pressing after it, and to exhort all others so to do.

"Q. What do we allow them?

"A. We grant—(1) That many of those who have died in the faith, yea the greater part of those we have known, were not perfected in love till a little before their death; (2) that the term *sanctified* is continually applied by St. Paul to all that were justified; (3) that by this term alone, he rarely, if ever, means, saved from all sin; (4) that, consequently, it is not proper to use it in that sense, without adding the word *wholly, entirely*, or the like; (5) that the inspired writers almost continually speak of or to those who were justified, but very rarely of or to those who were wholly sanctified;[1] (6) that, consequently, it behoves us to speak almost continually of the state of justification; but more rarely,[2] at least in full and explicit terms, concerning entire sanctification.

"Q. What, then, is the point where we divide?

"A. It is this: Should we expect to be saved from *all sin* before the article of death?

"Q. Is there any clear Scripture *promise* of this, that God will save us from *all sin*?

"A. There is: 'He shall redeem Israel from all his sins' (Psalm cxxx. 8).

"This is more largely expressed in the prophecy of Ezekiel: "Then will I sprinkle clean water upon you, and ye shall be clean: from all your filthiness and from all your idols, will I cleanse you,

---

[1] That is, unto those alone, exclusive of others. But they speak to them, jointly with others, almost continually.

[2] More rarely, I allow; but yet in some places very frequently, strongly, and explicitly.

I will also save you from all your uncleannesses' (ch. xxxiv. 25, 29). No promise can be more clear. And to this the apostle plainly refers in that exhortation, 'Having these promises, let us cleanse ourselves from all filthiness of flesh and spirit, perfecting holiness in the fear of God' (2 Cor. vii. 1). Equally clear and express is that ancient promise, 'The Lord thy God will circumcise thy heart, and the heart of thy seed, to love the Lord thy God with all thy heart and with all thy soul' (Deut. xxx. 6).

"Q. But does any assertion answerable to this occur in the New Testament?

"A. There does: and that laid down in the plainest terms. So, 1 John iii. 8: 'For this purpose the Son of God was manifested, that He might destroy the works of the devil'; the works of the devil without any limitation or restriction; but all sin is the work of the devil. Parallel to which is the assertion of St. Paul, Eph. v. 25–27: 'Christ loved the church, and gave Himself for it; that He might present it to Himself a glorious church, not having spot, or wrinkle, or any such thing: but that it might be holy and without blemish.'

"And to the same effect is his assertion in the eighth of the Romans (ver. 3, 4): 'God sent His Son,—that the righteousness of the law might be fulfilled in us, who walk not after the flesh, but after the Spirit.'

"Q. Does the New Testament afford

any further ground for expecting to be saved from *all sin*?

"A. Undoubtedly it does, both in those *prayers* and *commands*, which are equivalent to the strongest assertions.

"Q. What prayers do you mean?

"A. Prayers for entire sanctification, which, were there no such thing, would be mere mockery of God. Such, in particular, are—(1) 'Deliver us from evil.' Now, when this is done, when we are delivered from all evil, there can be no sin remaining. (2) 'Neither pray I for these alone, but for them also who shall believe on Me through their word; that they all may be one; as Thou, Father, art in Me, and I in Thee, that they also may be one in Us; I in them, and Thou in Me, that they may be made perfect in one' (John xvii. 20-23). (3) 'I bow my knees unto the God and Father of our Lord Jesus Christ, that He would grant you, that ye, being rooted and grounded in love, may be able to comprehend with all saints what is the breadth, and length, and depth, and height; and to know the love of Christ, which passeth knowledge, that ye might be filled with all the fulness of God' (Eph. iii. 14, etc.). (4) 'The very God of peace sanctify you wholly; and I pray God, your whole spirit, soul, and body may be preserved blameless unto the coming of our Lord Jesus Christ' (1 Thess. v. 23).

"Q. What command is there to the same effect?

"A. 1. 'Be ye perfect, as your Father

who is in heaven is perfect' (Matt. v. 48). 2. 'Thou shalt love the Lord thy God with all thy heart, and with all thy soul, and with all thy mind' (Matt. xxii. 37). But if the love of God fill *all the heart*, there can be no sin therein.

"Q. But how does it appear that this is to be done before the article of death?

"A. 1. From the very nature of a command, which is not given to the dead, but to the living. Therefore, 'Thou shalt love God with all thy heart,' cannot mean, Thou shalt do this when thou diest, but, while thou livest.

"2. From express texts of Scripture. (1) 'The grace of God that bringeth salvation hath appeared to all men, teaching us that, having renounced ungodliness and worldly lust, we should *live* soberly, righteously, and godly, in this present world; looking for the glorious appearing of our Lord Jesus Christ; who gave Himself for us, that He might redeem us from all iniquity, and purify unto Himself a peculiar people, zealous of good works' (Tit. ii. 11–14). (2) 'He hath raised up an horn of salvation for us, to perform the mercy promised to our fathers: the oath which he sware to our father Abraham, that He would grant unto us, that we being delivered out of the hands of our enemies should serve Him without fear, in holiness and righteousness before Him all the days of our life' (Luke i. 69, etc.).

"Q. Is there any example in Scripture of persons who had attained to this?

"A. Yes; St. John, and all those of whom he says, 'Herein is our love made perfect, that we may have boldness in the day of judgment: because as He is, so are we in this world' (1 John iv. 17).

"Q. Can you show one such example now? where is he that is thus perfect?

"A. To some that make this inquiry one might answer, If I knew one here, I would not tell you; for you do not inquire out of love. You are like Herod: you only seek the young child to slay it.

"But more directly we answer: There are many reasons why there should be few, if any, *indisputable* examples. What inconveniences would this bring on the person himself—set as a mark for all to shoot at! And how unprofitable would it be to gainsayers! 'For if they hear not Moses and the prophets,' Christ and His apostles, 'neither would they be persuaded though one rose from the dead.'

"Q. Are we not apt to have a secret distaste to any who say they are saved from all sin?

"A. It is very possible we may; and that upon several grounds: partly from a concern for the good of souls, who may be hurt if these are not what they profess; partly from a kind of explicit envy at those who speak of higher attainments than our own; and partly from our natural slowness and unreadiness of heart to believe the works of God.

"Q. Why may we not continue in the joy of faith till we are *perfected in love*?

"A. Why, indeed? since holy grief does not quench this joy; since even while we are under the cross, while we deeply partake of the sufferings of Christ, we may rejoice with joy unspeakable."

From these extracts it undeniably appears, not only what was mine and my brother's judgment, but what was the judgment of all the preachers in connection with us, in the years 1744, '45, '46, and '47. Nor do I remember, that in any one of these conferences we had one dissenting voice; but whatever doubts any one had when we met, they were all removed before we parted.

18. In the year 1749 my brother printed two volumes of *Hymns and Sacred Poems*. As I did not see these before they were published, there were some things in them which I did not approve of. But I quite approved of the main of the hymns on this head; a few verses of which are subjoined:—

"Come, Lord, be manifested here,
    And ALL the devil's works destroy;
Now, without sin, in me appear,
    And fill with everlasting joy;
Thy beatific face display,
Thy presence is the perfect day."
(Vol. i. p. 203.)

"Swift to my rescue come,
    Thy own this moment seize;
Gather my wandering spirit home,
    And keep in perfect peace:
Suffer'd no more to rove
    O'er all the earth abroad,
Arrest the prisoner of Thy love,
    And shut me up in God." (P. 247.)

"Thy prisoners release, vouchsafe us Thy peace;
And our sorrows and sins in a moment shall cease.
That moment be now! our petition allow,
Our present Redeemer and Comforter Thou!"
(Vol. ii. p. 124.)

"From this inbred sin deliver;
 Let the yoke now be broke;
   Make me Thine for ever.

Partner of Thy perfect nature,
 Let me be now in Thee
   A new, sinless creature." (P. 156.)

"Turn me, Lord, and turn me now,
 To Thy yoke my spirit bow;
 Grant me now the pearl to find
 Of a meek and quiet mind.

Calm, O calm my troubled breast;
 Let me gain that second rest;
 From my works for ever cease,
 Perfected in holiness." (P. 162.)

"Come in this accepted hour,
   Bring Thy heavenly kingdom in;
 Fill us with the glorious power,
   Rooting out the seeds of sin." (P. 168.)

"Come, thou dear Lamb, for sinners slain,
   Bring in the cleansing flood:
 Apply, to wash out every stain,
   Thine efficacious blood.
 O let it sink into our soul
   Deep as the inbred sin;
 Make every wounded spirit whole,
   And every leper clean!" (P. 171.)

"Prisoners of hope, arise,
   And see your Lord appear;
 Lo! on the wings of love He flies,
   And brings redemption near.
 Redemption in His blood
   He calls you to receive:
'Come unto Me, the pardoning God
   Believe,' He cries, 'believe!'

> Jesus, to Thee we look,
> Till saved from sin's remains,
> Reject the inbred tyrant's yoke,
> And cast away his chains.
> Our nature shall no more
> O'er us dominion have;
> By faith we apprehend the power
> Which shall for ever save." (P. 188.)

> "Jesu, our life, in us appear,
> Who daily die Thy death:
> Reveal Thyself the Finisher;
> Thy quick'ning Spirit breathe!
> Unfold the hidden mystery,
> The second gift impart;
> Reveal Thy glorious Self in me,
> In every waiting heart." (P. 195.)

"In Him we have peace, in Him we have power;
Preserved by His grace, throughout the dark hour;
In all our temptation He keeps us to prove
His utmost salvation, His fulness of love.

Pronounce the glad word, and bid us be free!
Ah, hast Thou not, Lord, a blessing for me?
The peace Thou hast given, this moment impart,
And open Thy heaven, O Love, in my heart."
(P. 324.)

A second edition of these hymns was published in the year 1752; and that without any other alteration than that of a few literal mistakes.

I have been the more large in these extracts, because hence it appears, beyond all possibility of exception, that to this day both my brother and I maintained— (1) That Christian perfection is that love of God and our neighbour which implies deliverance from *all sin*; (2) that this is received merely *by faith*; (3) that it is given *instantaneously,* in one moment; (4) that we are to expect it, not at death, but *every moment*; that *now* is the accepted time, *now* is the day of this salvation.

19. At the conference in the year 1759, perceiving some danger that a diversity of sentiments should insensibly steal in among us, we again largely considered this doctrine. And soon after I published *Thoughts on Christian Perfection,* prefaced with the following advertisement:—

"The following tract is by no means designed to gratify the curiosity of any man. It is not intended to prove the doctrine at large, in opposition to those who explode and ridicule it; no, nor to answer the numerous objections against it which may be raised even by serious men. All I intend here is simply to declare what are my sentiments on this head; what Christian perfection does, according to my apprehension, include, and what it does not; and to add a few practical observations and directions relative to the subject.

"As these thoughts were at first thrown together by way of question and answer, I let them continue in the same form. They are just the same that I have entertained for above twenty years.

"Q. What is Christian Perfection?

"A. The loving God with all our heart, mind, soul, and strength. This implies that no wrong temper, none contrary to love, remains in the soul; and that all the thoughts, words, and actions are governed by pure love.

4

"Q. Do you affirm that this perfection excludes all infirmities, ignorance, and mistake?

"A. I continually affirm quite the contrary, and always have done so.

"Q. But how can every thought, word, and work be governed by pure love, and the man be subject at the same time to ignorance and mistake?

"A. I see no contradiction here: 'A man may be filled with pure love, and still be liable to mistake.' Indeed, I do not expect to be freed from actual mistakes till this mortal puts on immortality. I believe this to be a natural consequence of the soul's dwelling in flesh and blood. For we cannot now *think* at all, but by the mediation of those bodily organs, which have suffered equally with the rest of our frame. And hence we cannot avoid sometimes *thinking wrong*, till this corruptible shall have put on incorruption.

"But we may carry this thought farther yet. A mistake in judgment may possibly occasion a mistake in practice. For instance: Mr. De Renty's mistake touching the nature of mortification, arising from prejudice of education, occasioned that practical mistake, his wearing an iron girdle. And a thousand such instances there may be, even in those who are in the highest state of grace. Yet, where every word and action springs from love, such a mistake is not properly *a sin*. However, it cannot bear the rigour of God's justice, but needs the atoning blood.

"Q. What was the judgment of all our brethren who met at Bristol, in August 1758, on this head?

"A. It was expressed in these words: (1) Every one may mistake as long as he lives. (2) A mistake in *opinion* may occasion a mistake in *practice*. (3) Every such mistake is a transgression of the perfect law. Therefore (4) Every such mistake, were it not for the blood of atonement, would expose to eternal damnation. (5) It follows that the most perfect have continual need of the merits of Christ, even for their actual transgressions, and may say, for themselves, as well as for their brethren, 'Forgive us our trespasses.'

"This easily accounts for what might otherwise seem to be utterly unaccountable, namely, that those who are not offended when we speak of the highest degree of love, yet will not hear of living *without sin*. The reason is, they know, all men are liable to mistake, and that in practice as well as in judgment. But they do not know, or do not observe, that this is not sin, if love is the sole principle of action.

"Q. But still if they live without sin, does not this exclude the necessity of a Mediator? At least, is it not plain that they stand no longer in need of Christ in His priestly office?

"A. Far from it. None feel their need of Christ like these; none so entirely depend upon Him. For Christ does not give life to the soul separate from, but in and with, Himself. Hence his words are equally true of all men, in whatsoever state of grace they are: 'As the branch cannot bear fruit of itself, except it abide in the vine; no more can ye, except ye abide in Me. Without' (or separate from) 'Me ye can do nothing.'

"In every state we need Christ in the following respects:—(1) Whatever grace we receive, it is a free gift from Him. (2) We receive it as His purchase, merely in consideration of the price He paid. (3) We have this grace, not only from Christ, but in Him. For our perfection is not like that of a tree, which flourishes by the sap derived from its own root, but, as was said before, like that of a branch, which, united to the vine, bears fruit; but, severed from it, is dried up and withered. (4) All our blessings, temporal, spiritual, and eternal, depend on His intercession for us, which is one branch of His priestly office, whereof therefore we have always equal need. (5) The best of men still need Christ, in His priestly office, to atone for their omissions, their shortcomings (as some not improperly speak), their mistakes in judgment and practice, and their defects of various kinds, for these are all deviations from the perfect law, and consequently need an atonement. Yet that they are not properly sins, we apprehend, may appear from the words of St Paul: 'He that loveth hath fulfilled the law; for love is the fulfilling of the law' (Rom. xiii. 10). Now, mistakes and whatever infirmities necessarily flow from the corruptible state of the body are no way contrary to love; nor therefore, in the Scripture sense, sin.

"To explain myself a little farther on this head—(1) Not only sin, properly so called (that is, a voluntary transgression of a known law), but sin, improperly so called (that is, an involuntary transgression of a divine law, known or unknown), needs the atoning blood. (2) I believe there is no such perfection in this life as excludes these involuntary transgressions, which I apprehend to be naturally consequent on the ignorance and mistakes inseparable from mortality. (3) Therefore, *sinless perfection* is a phrase I never use, lest I should seem to contradict myself. (4) I believe, a person filled with the love of God is still liable to these involuntary transgressions. (5) Such transgressions you may call sins, if you please: I do not, for the reasons above mentioned.

"Q. What advice would you give to those that do, and those that do not, call them so?

"A. Let those that do not call them sins never think that themselves or any other persons are in such a state as that they can stand before infinite justice without a Mediator. This must argue either the deepest ignorance, or the highest arrogance and presumption.

"Let those who do call them so, beware how they confound these defects with sins, properly so called.

"But how will they avoid it? how will these be distinguished from those, if they are all promiscuously called sins? I am much afraid, if we should allow any sins to be consistent with perfection, few would confine the idea to those defects concerning which only the assertion could be true.

"Q. But how can a liableness to mistake consist with perfect love? Is not a person who is perfected in love every moment under its influence? And can any mistake flow from pure love?

"A. I answer—(1) Many mistakes may consist with pure love. (2) Some may accidentally flow from it: I mean, love itself may incline us to mistake. The pure love of our neighbour, springing from the love of God, thinketh no evil, believeth and hopeth all things. Now, this very temper, unsuspicious, ready to believe and hope the best of all men, may occasion our thinking some men better than they really are. Here, then, is a manifest mistake, accidentally flowing from pure love.

"Q. How shall we avoid setting perfection too high or too low?

"A. By keeping to the Bible, and setting it just as high as the Scripture does. It is nothing higher and nothing lower than this—the pure love of God and man; the loving God with all our heart and soul, and our neighbour as ourselves. It is love governing the heart and life, running through all our tempers, words, and actions.

"Q. Suppose one had attained to this, would you advise him to speak of it?

"A. At first, perhaps, he would scarce be able to refrain, the fire would be so hot within him; his desire to declare the loving-kindness of the Lord carrying him away like a torrent. But afterwards he might: and then it would be advisable not to speak of it to them that know not God (it is most likely it would only provoke them to contradict and blaspheme); nor to others, without some particular reason, without some good in view. And then he should have especial care to avoid all appearance of boasting; to speak with the deepest humility and reverence, giving all the glory to God.

"Q. But would it not be better to be entirely silent, not to speak of it at all?

"A. By silence he might avoid many crosses, which will naturally and necessarily ensue, if he simply declare, even among believers, what God has wrought in his soul. If, therefore, such a one were to confer with flesh and blood, he would be entirely silent. But this could not be done with a clear conscience; for undoubtedly he ought to speak. Men do not light a candle to put it under a bushel: much less does the all-wise God. He does not raise such a monument of His power and love, to hide it from all mankind: rather He intends it as a general blessing to those who are simple of heart. He designs thereby not barely the happiness of that individual person, but the animating and encouraging others to follow after the same blessing. His will is, 'that many shall see it' and rejoice, 'and put their trust in the Lord.' Nor does anything under heaven more quicken the desires of those who are justified, than to converse with those whom they believe to have experienced a still higher salvation. This places that salvation full in their view, and increases their hunger and thirst after it: an advantage which must have been entirely lost, had the person so saved buried himself in silence.

"Q. But is there no way to prevent these crosses which usually fall on those who speak of being thus saved?

"A. It seems they cannot be prevented altogether, while so much of nature remains even in believers. But something might be done, if the preacher in every place would (1) talk freely with all who speak thus, and (2) labour to prevent the unjust or unkind treatment of those, in favour of whom there is reasonable proof.

"Q. What is reasonable proof? How may we certainly know one that is saved from all sin?

"A. We cannot infallibly know one that is thus saved (no, nor even one that is justified), unless it should please God to endow us with the miraculous discernment of spirits. But we apprehend these would be sufficient proofs to any reasonable man, and such as would leave little room to doubt either the truth or depth of the work—(1) If we had clear evidence of his exemplary behaviour for some time before this supposed change. This would give us reason to believe he would not 'lie for God,' but speak neither more nor less than he felt. (2) If he gave a distinct account of the time and manner wherein the change was wrought, with sound speech which could not be reproved. And (3) if it appeared that all his subsequent words and actions were holy and unblamable.

"The short of the matter is this—(1) I have abundant reason to believe this person will not lie; (2) he testifies before God, 'I feel no sin, but all love; I pray, rejoice, and give thanks without ceasing; and I have as clear an inward witness that I am fully renewed, as that I am justified.' Now, if I have nothing to oppose to this plain testimony, I ought in reason to believe it.

"It avails nothing to object, 'But I know several things wherein he is quite mistaken.' For it has been allowed that all who are in the body are liable to mistake, and that a mistake in judgment may sometimes occasion a mistake in practice; though great care is to be taken that no ill use be made of this concession. For instance: Even one that is perfected in love may mistake with regard to another person, and may think him, in a particular case, to be more or less faulty than he really is; and hence he may speak to him with more or less severity than the truth requires. And in this sense (though that be not the primary meaning of St. James), 'in many things we offend all.' This therefore is no proof at all that the person so speaking is not perfect.

"Q. But is it not a proof, if he is surprised or fluttered by a noise, a fall, or some sudden danger?

"A. It is not; for one may start, tremble, change colour, or be otherwise disordered in body, while the soul is calmly stayed on God, and remains in perfect peace. Nay, the mind itself may be deeply distressed, may be exceeding sorrowful, may be perplexed and pressed down by heaviness and anguish, even to agony, while the heart cleaves to God by perfect love, and the will is wholly resigned to Him. Was it not so with the Son of God Himself? Does any child of man endure the distress, the anguish, the agony, which He sustained? And yet He knew no sin.

"Q. But can any one who has a pure heart prefer pleasing to unpleasing food, or use any pleasure of sense which is not strictly necessary? If so, how do they differ from others?

"A. The difference between these and others in taking pleasant food is—(1) They need none of these things to make them happy; for they have a spring of happiness within. They see and love God. Hence they rejoice evermore, and in everything give thanks. (2) They may use them, but they do not seek them. (3) They use them sparingly, and not for the sake of the thing itself. This being premised, we answer directly—Such a one may use pleasing food without the danger which attends those who are not saved from sin. He may prefer it to unpleasing, though equally wholesome, food, as a means of increasing thankfulness, with a single eye to God, who giveth us all things richly to enjoy. On the same principle, he may smell to a flower, or eat a bunch of grapes, or take any other pleasure which does not lessen but increase his delight in God. Therefore, neither can we say that one perfected in love would be incapable of marriage, and of worldly business—if he were called thereto, he would be more capable than ever; as being able to do all things without hurry or carefulness, without any distraction of spirit.

"Q. But if two perfect Christians had children, how could they be born in sin, since there was none in the parents?

"A. It is a possible, but not a probable, case; I doubt whether it ever was, or ever will be. But, waiving this, I answer, Sin is entailed upon me, not by immediate generation, but by my first parent. 'In Adam all died; by the disobedience of one, all men were made sinners'; all men, without exception, who were in his loins when he ate the forbidden fruit.

"We have a remarkable illustration of this in gardening: grafts on a crab-stock bear excellent fruit; but sow the kernels of this fruit, and what will be the event? They produce as mere crabs as ever were eaten.

"Q. But what does the perfect one do more than others? more than the common believers?

"A. Perhaps nothing; so may the providence of God have hedged him in by outward circumstances. Perhaps not so much; though he desires and longs to spend and be spent for God—at least, not externally; he neither speaks so many words, nor does so many works; as neither did our Lord Himself speak so many words, or do so many, no, nor so great works, as some of His apostles (John xiv. 12). But what then? This is no proof that he has not more grace; and by this God measures the outward work. Hear ye Him: 'Verily I say unto you, This poor widow has cast in more than they all.' Verily, this poor man, with his few broken words, hath spoken more than they all. Verily, this poor woman, that hath given a cup of cold water, hath done more than they all. Oh, cease to 'judge according to appearance,' and learn to 'judge righteous judgment!'

"Q. But is not this a proof against him,—I feel no power either in his words or prayer?

"A. It is not; for perhaps that is your own fault. You are not likely to feel any power therein, if any of these hindrances lie in the way—(1) Your own deadness of soul. The dead Pharisees felt no power even in His words who 'spake as never man spake.' (2) The guilt of some unrepented sin lying upon the conscience. (3) Prejudice toward him of any kind. (4) Your not believing that state to be attainable wherein he professes to be. (5) Unreadiness to think or own he has attained it. (6) Overvaluing or idolising him. (7) Overvaluing yourself and your own judgment. If any of these is the case, what wonder is it that you feel no power in anything he says? But do not others feel it? If they do, your argument falls to the ground. And if they do not, do none of these hindrances lie in their way too? You must be certain of this before you can build any argument thereon; and even then your argument will prove no more than that grace and gifts do not always go together.

"'But he does not come up to my idea of a perfect Christian.' And perhaps no one ever did, or ever will. For your idea may go beyond, or at least beside, the scriptural account. It may include more than the Bible includes therein; or, however, something which that does not include. Scripture perfection is pure love, filling the heart, and governing all the words and actions. If your idea includes anything more or anything else, it is not scriptural; and then, no wonder that a scripturally perfect Christian does not come up to it.

"I fear many stumble on this stumbling-block. They include as many ingredients as they please, not according to Scripture, but their own imagination, in their idea of one that is perfect; and then readily deny any one to be such who does not answer that imaginary idea.

"The more care should we take to keep the simple scriptural account continually in our eye. Pure love reigning alone in the heart and life, this is the whole of scriptural perfection.

"Q. When may a person judge himself to have attained this?

"A. When, after having been fully convinced of inbred sin, by a far deeper and clearer conviction than that he experienced before justification, and after having experienced a gradual mortification of it, he experiences a total death to sin, and an entire renewal in the love and image of God, so as to rejoice evermore, to pray without ceasing, and in everything to give thanks. Not that 'to feel all love and no sin' is a sufficient proof. Several have experienced this for a time, before their souls were fully renewed. None therefore ought to believe that the work is done, till there is added the testimony of the Spirit witnessing his entire sanctification as clearly as his justification.

"Q. But whence is it that some imagine they are thus sanctified, when in reality they are not?

"A. It is hence: they do not judge by all the preceding marks, but either by part of them, or by others that are ambiguous. But I know no instance of a person attending to them all, and yet deceived in this matter. I believe there can be none in the world. If a man be deeply and fully convinced, after justification, of inbred sin; if he then experience a gradual mortification of sin, and afterwards an entire renewal in the image of God; if to this change, immensely greater than that wrought when he was justified, be added a clear direct witness of the renewal, I judge it as impossible this man should be deceived herein, as that God should lie. And if one whom I know to be a man of veracity testify these things to me, I ought not, without some sufficient reason, to reject his testimony.

"Q. Is this death to sin, and renewal in love, gradual or instantaneous?

"A. A man may be dying for some time; yet he does not, properly speaking, die till the instant the soul is separated from the body; and in that instant he lives the life of eternity. In like manner, he may be dying to sin for some time; yet he is not dead to sin till sin is separated from his soul; and in that instant he lives the full life of love. And as the change undergone when the body dies is of a different kind, and infinitely greater than any we had known before, yea, such as till then it is impossible to conceive; so the change wrought when the soul dies to sin is of a different kind, and infinitely greater than any before, and than any can conceive till he experiences it. Yet he still grows in grace, in the knowledge of Christ, in the love and image of God; and will do so, not only till death, but to all eternity.

"Q. How are we to wait for this change?

"A. Not in careless indifference, or indolent inactivity; but in vigorous, universal obedience, in a zealous keeping of all the commandments, in watchfulness and painfulness, in denying ourselves, and taking up our cross daily; as well as in earnest prayer and fasting, and a close attendance on all the ordinances of God. And if any man dream of attaining it any other way (yea, or of keeping it when it is attained, when he has received it even in the largest measure), he deceiveth his own soul. It is true, we receive it by simple faith; but God does not, will not, give that faith unless we seek it with all diligence, in the way which He hath ordained.

"This consideration may satisfy those who inquire, why so few have received the blessing. Inquire how many are seeking it in this way; and you have a sufficient answer.

"Prayer especially is wanting. Who continues instant therein? Who wrestles with God for this very thing? So, 'ye have not, because ye ask not; or because ye ask amiss,' namely, that you may be renewed before you die. *Before you die!* Will that content you? Nay, but ask that it may be done now; to-day, while it is called to-day. Do not call this 'setting God a time.' Certainly, to-day is His time as well as to-morrow. Make haste, man, make haste. Let

> 'Thy soul break out in strong desire,
>   The perfect bliss to prove;
> Thy longing heart be all on fire
>   To be dissolved in love!'

"Q. But may we not continue in peace and joy till we are perfected in love?

"A. Certainly we may; for the kingdom of God is not divided against itself; therefore let not believers be discouraged from 'rejoicing in the Lord always.' And yet we may be sensibly pained at the sinful nature that still remains in us. It is good for us to have a piercing sense of this, and a vehement desire to be delivered from it. But this should only incite us the more zealously to fly every moment to our strong Helper; the more earnestly to 'press forward to the mark, the prize of our high calling in Christ Jesus.' And when the sense of our sin most abounds, the sense of His love should much more abound.

"Q. How should we treat those who think they have attained?

"A. Examine them candidly, and exhort them to pray fervently that God would show them all that is in their hearts. The most earnest exhortations to abound in every grace, and the strongest cautions to avoid all evil, are given throughout the New Testament to those who are in the highest state of grace. But this should be done with the utmost tenderness, and without any harshness, sternness, or sourness. We should carefully avoid the very appearance of anger, unkindness, or contempt. Leave it to Satan thus to tempt, and to his children to cry out, 'Let us examine him with despitefulness and torture, that we may know his meekness and prove his patience.' If they are faithful to the grace given, they are in no danger of perishing thereby; no, not if they remain in that mistake till their spirit is returning to God.

"Q. But what hurt can it do to deal harshly with them?

"A. Either they are mistaken, or they are not. If they are, it may destroy their souls. This is nothing impossible, no, nor improbable. It may so enrage or so discourage them, that they will sink and rise no more. If they are not mistaken, it may grieve those whom God has not grieved, and do much hurt unto our own souls. For undoubtedly he that toucheth them, toucheth, as it were, the apple of God's eye. If they are indeed full of His Spirit, to behave unkindly or contemptuously to them is doing no little despite to the Spirit of grace. Hereby, likewise, we feed and increase in ourselves evil surmising, and many wrong tempers. To instance only in one: What self-sufficiency is this, to set ourselves up for inquisitors-general, for peremptory judges in these deep things of God! Are we qualified for the office? Can we pronounce in all cases, how far infirmity reaches? what may, and what may not, be resolved into it? what may in all circumstances, and what may not, consist with perfect love? Can we precisely determine how it will influence the look, the gesture, the tone of voice? If we can, doubtless we are 'the men, and wisdom shall die with us.'

"Q. But if they are displeased at our not believing them, is not this a full proof against them?

"A. According as that displeasure is: if they are angry, it is a proof against them; if they are grieved, it is not. They ought to be grieved, if we disbelieve a real work of God, and thereby deprive ourselves of the advantage we might have received from it. And we may easily mistake this grief for anger, as the outward expressions of both are much alike.

"Q. But it is not well to find out those who fancy they have attained when they have not?

"A. It is well to do it by mild, loving examination. But it is not well to triumph even over these. It is extremely wrong, if we find such an instance, to rejoice as if we had found great spoils. Ought we not rather to grieve, to be deeply concerned, to let our eyes run down with tears? Here is one who seemed to be a living proof of God's power, to save to the uttermost; but, alas! it is not as we hoped. He is weighed in the balance, and found wanting. And is this matter of joy? Ought we not to rejoice a thousand times more, if we can find nothing but pure love?

"'But he is deceived.' What then? It is a harmless mistake, while he feels nothing but love in his heart. It is a mistake which generally argues great grace, a high degree both of holiness and happiness. This should be a matter of real joy to all that are simple of heart: not the mistake itself, but the height of grace which for a time occasions it. I rejoice that this soul is always happy in Christ, always full of prayer and thanksgiving. I rejoice that he feels no unholy temper, but the pure love of God continually. And I will rejoice, if sin is suspended till it is totally destroyed.

"Q. Is there no danger, then, in a man's being thus deceived?

"A. Not at the time that he feels no sin. There was danger before, and there will be again when he comes into fresh trials. But so long as he feels nothing but love animating all his thoughts, and words, and actions, he is in no danger: he is not only happy, but safe, 'under the shadow of the Almighty'; and for God's sake, let him continue in that love as long as he can. Meantime you may do well to warn him of the danger that will be, if his love grow cold and sin revive: even the danger of casting away hope, and supposing that, because he hath not attained yet, therefore he never shall.

"Q. But what if none have attained it yet? What if all who think so are deceived?

"A. Convince me of this, and I will preach it no more. But understand me right: I do not build any doctrine on this or that person. This or any other man may be deceived, and I am not moved. But if there are none made perfect yet, God has not sent me to preach perfection.

"Put a parallel case: For many years I have preached, 'There is a peace of God which passeth all understanding.' Convince me that this word has fallen to the ground; that in all these years none have attained this peace; that there is no living witness of it at this day; and I will preach it no more.

"'Oh, but several persons have died in that peace.' Perhaps so; but I want living witnesses. I cannot indeed be infallibly certain that this or that person is a witness; but if I were certain there are none such, I must have done with this doctrine.

"'You misunderstand me. I believe some who died in this love, enjoyed it long before their death. But I was not certain that their former testimony was true till some hours before they died.'

"You had not an infallible certainty then: and a reasonable certainty you might have had before; such a certainty as might have quickened and comforted your own soul, and answered all other Christian purposes. Such a certainty as this any candid person may have, suppose there be any living witness, by talking one hour with that person in the love and fear of God.

"Q. But what does it signify whether any have attained it or no, seeing so many scriptures witness for it?

"A. If I were convinced that none in England had attained what has been so clearly and strongly preached by such a number of preachers in so many places, and for so long a time, I should be clearly convinced that we had all mistaken the meaning of those scriptures; and therefore, for the time to come, I too must teach that 'sin will remain till death.'"

20. In the year 1762 there was a great increase of the work of God in London. Many, who had hitherto cared for none of these things, were deeply convinced of their lost estate; many found redemption in the blood of Christ; not a few backsliders were healed; and a considerable number of persons believed that God had

saved them from all sin. Easily foreseeing that Satan would be endeavouring to sow tares among the wheat, I took much pains to apprise them of the danger, particularly with regard to pride and enthusiasm. And while I stayed in town, I had reason to hope they continued both humble and sober-minded. But almost as soon as I was gone, enthusiasm broke in. Two or three began to take their own imaginations for impressions from God, and thence to suppose that they should never die; and these, labouring to bring others into the same opinion, occasioned much noise and confusion. Soon after, the same persons, with a few more, ran into other extravagances,—fancying they could not be tempted; that they should feel no more pain; and that they had the gift of prophecy, and of discerning of spirits. At my return to London, in autumn, some of them stood reproved; but others were got above instruction. Meantime a flood of reproach came upon me almost from every quarter: from themselves, because I was checking them on all occasions; and from others, because, they said, I did not check them. However, the hand of the Lord was not stayed, but more and more sinners were convinced; while some were almost daily converted to God, and others enabled to love Him with all their heart.

21. About this time, a friend at some distance from London wrote to me as follows:—

"Be not over-alarmed that Satan sows tares among the wheat of Christ. It ever has been so, especially on any remarkable outpouring of His Spirit; and ever will be so, till he is chained up for a thousand years. Till then he will always ape, and endeavour to counteract, the work of the Spirit of Christ.

"One melancholy effect of this has been, that a world, who is always asleep in the arms of the evil one, has ridiculed every work of the Holy Spirit.

"But what can real Christians do? Why, if they would act worthy of themselves, they should—(1) Pray that every deluded soul may be delivered; (2) endeavour to reclaim them in the spirit of meekness; and, lastly, take the utmost care, both by prayer and watchfulness, that the delusion of others may not lessen their zeal in seeking after that universal holiness of soul, body and spirit, 'without which no man shall see the Lord.'

"Indeed, this complete new creature is mere madness to a mad world. But it is, notwithstanding, the will and wisdom of God. May we all seek after it!

"But some who maintain this doctrine in its full extent are too often guilty of limiting the Almighty. He dispenses His gifts just as He pleases; therefore it is neither wise nor modest to affirm that a person must be a believer for any length of time before he is capable of receiving a high degree of the Spirit of holiness.

"God's usual method is one thing, but His sovereign pleasure is another. He has wise reasons both for hastening and retarding His work. Sometimes He comes suddenly, and unexpected; sometimes, not till we have long looked for Him.

"Indeed it has been my opinion for many years, that one great cause why men make so little improvement in the divine life is their own coldness, negligence, and unbelief. And yet I here speak of believers.

"May the Spirit of Christ give us a right judgment in all things, and 'fill us with all the fulness of God'; that so we may be 'perfect and entire, wanting nothing.'"

22. About the same time, five or six honest enthusiasts foretold the world was to end on the 28th of February. I immediately withstood them, by every possible means, both in public and private. I preached expressly upon the subject, both at West Street and Spitalfields. I warned the Society again and again, and spoke severally to as many as I could. And I saw the fruit of my labour. They made exceeding few converts; I believe scarce thirty in our whole Society. Nevertheless, they made abundance of noise; gave huge occasion of offence to those who took care to improve to the uttermost every occasion against me; and greatly increased both the number and courage of those who opposed Christian perfection.

23. Some questions, now published by one of these, induced a plain man to write the following:—

"QUERIES humbly proposed to those

who deny perfection to be attainable in this life.

"(1) Has there not been a larger measure of the Holy Spirit given under the Gospel than under the Jewish dispensation? If not, in what sense was the Spirit not given before Christ was glorified? (John vii. 39).

"(2) Was that 'glory which followed the sufferings of Christ' (1 Peter i. 11) an external glory, or an internal, viz., the glory of holiness?

"(3) Has God anywhere in Scripture commanded us more than He has promised to us?

"(4) Are the promises of God respecting holiness to be fulfilled in this life, or only in the next?

"(5) Is a Christian under any other laws than those which God promises to 'write in our hearts'? (Jer. xxxi. 31, etc.; Heb. viii. 10).

"(6) In what sense is 'the righteousness of the law fulfilled in those who walk not after the flesh, but after the Spirit'? (Romans viii. 4).

"(7) Is it impossible for any one in this life to love God 'with all his heart, and mind, and soul, and strength'? And is the Christian under any law which is not fulfilled in this love?

"(8) Does the soul's going out of the body effect its purification from indwelling sin?

"(9) If so, is it not something else, not 'the blood of Christ, which cleanseth' it 'from all sin'?

"(10) If His blood cleanseth us from all sin, while the soul and body are united, is it not in this life?

"(11) If when that union ceases, is it not in the next? And is not this too late?

"(12) If in the article of death; what situation is the soul in, when it is neither in the body nor out of it?

"(13) Has Christ anywhere taught us to pray for what He never designs to give?

"(14) Has He not taught us to pray, 'Thy will be done on earth, as it is done in heaven'? And is it not done perfectly in heaven?

"(15) If so, has He not taught us to pray for perfection on earth? Does He not then design to give it?

"(16) Did not St. Paul pray according to the will of God, when he prayed that the Thessalonians might be 'sanctified wholly, and preserved' (in this world, not the next, unless he was praying for the dead) 'blameless in body, soul, and spirit, unto the coming of Jesus Christ'?

"(17) Do you sincerely desire to be freed from indwelling sin in this life?

"(18) If you do, did not God give you that desire?

"(19) If so, did He not give it you to mock you, since it is impossible it should ever be fulfilled?

"(20) If you have not sincerity enough even to desire it, are you not disputing about matters too high for you?

"(21) Do you ever pray God to 'cleanse

the thoughts of your heart, that' you 'may perfectly love Him'?

"(22) If you neither desire what you ask, nor believe it attainable, pray you not as a fool prayeth?

"God help thee to consider these questions calmly and impartially!"

24. In the latter end of this year God called to Himself that burning and shining light, Jane Cooper. As she was both a living and a dying witness of Christian perfection, it will not be at all foreign to the subject to add a short account of her death; with one of her own letters, containing a plain and artless relation of the manner wherein it pleased God to work that great change in her soul:—

"*May* 2, 1761.

"I BELIEVE while memory remains in me, gratitude will continue. From the time you preached on Gal. v. 5, I saw clearly the true state of my soul. That sermon described my heart, and what it wanted to be, namely, truly happy. You read Mr. M—'s letter, and it described the religion which I desired. From that time the prize appeared in view, and I was enabled to follow hard after it. I was kept watching unto prayer, sometimes in much distress, at other times in patient expectation of the blessing. For some days before you left London, my soul was stayed on a promise I had applied to me in prayer: 'The Lord whom ye seek shall suddenly come to His temple.' I believed He would, and that He would sit there as a refiner's fire. The Tuesday after you went, I thought I could not sleep, unless He fulfilled His word that night. I never knew as I did then the force of these words: 'Be still, and know that I am God.' I became nothing before Him, and enjoyed perfect calmness in my soul. I knew not whether He had destroyed my sin; but I desired to know, that I might praise Him. Yet I soon found the return of unbelief, and groaned, being burdened. On Wednesday I went to London, and sought the Lord without ceasing. I promised, if He would save me from sin, I would praise Him. I could part with all things, so I might win Christ. But I found all these pleas to be nothing worth; and that if He saved me, it must be freely, for His own Name's sake. On Thursday I was so much tempted, that I thought of destroying myself, or never conversing more with the people of God; and yet I had no doubt of His pardoning love; but

> ''Twas worse than death my God to love,
> And not my God alone.'

On Friday my distress was deepened. I endeavoured to pray, and could not. I went to Mrs. D., who prayed for me, and told me it was the death of nature. I opened the Bible on, 'The fearful, and unbelieving, shall have their part in the lake which burneth with fire and brimstone.' I could not bear it. I opened again on Mark xvi. 6, 7: 'Be not affrighted: ye seek Jesus of Nazareth.

Go your way, tell His disciples He goeth before you into Galilee: there shall ye see Him.' I was encouraged and enabled to pray, believing I should see Jesus at home. I returned that night, and found Mrs. G. She prayed for me; and the predestinarian had no plea, but, 'Lord, Thou art no respecter of persons.' He proved He was not, by blessing me. I was in a moment enabled to lay hold on Jesus Christ, and found salvation by simple faith. He assured me, the Lord, the King was in the midst of me, and that I should see evil no more. I now blessed Him, who had visited and redeemed me, and was become my 'wisdom, righteousness, sanctification, and redemption.' I saw Jesus altogether lovely; and knew He was mine in all His offices. And glory be to Him, He now reigns in my heart without a rival. I find no will but His. I feel no pride; nor any affection but what is placed on Him. I know it is by faith I stand; and that watching unto prayer must be the guard of faith. I am happy in God at this moment, and I believe for the next. I have often read the chapter you mention (1 Cor. xiii.), and compared my heart and life with it. In so doing, I feel my shortcomings and the need I have of the atoning blood. Yet I dare not say I do not feel a measure of the love there described, though I am not all I shall be. I desire to be lost in that 'love which passeth knowledge.' I see 'the just shall live by faith'; and unto me, who am less than the least of all saints, is this **grace** given. If I were an archangel, I should veil my face before Him, and let silence speak His praise."

The following account is given by one who was an eye and ear witness of what she relates :—

"(1) In the beginning of November she seemed to have a foresight of what was coming upon her, and used frequently to sing these words—

' When pain o'er this weak flesh prevails,
With lamb-like patience arm my breast.'

And when she sent to me, to let me know she was ill, she wrote in her note, ' I suffer the will of Jesus. All He sends is sweetened by His love. I am as happy as if I heard a voice say—

" ' For me my elder brethren stay,
And angels beckon me away,
And Jesus bids me come." '

"(2) Upon my telling her, 'I cannot choose life or death for you,' she said, 'I asked the Lord, that, if it was His will, I might die first. And He told me you should survive me, and that you should close my eyes.' When we perceived it was the small-pox, I said to her, 'My dear, you will not be frighted if we tell you what is your distemper.' She said, 'I cannot be frighted at His will.'

"(3) The distemper was soon very heavy upon her; but so much the more was her faith strengthened. Tuesday, November 16, she said to me, 'I have been worshipping before the throne in a glorious manner; my soul was so let into God!' I said, 'Did the Lord give you any particular promise?' 'No,' replied she; 'it was all

> "That sacred awe that dares not move,
> And all the silent heaven of love."'

"(4) On Thursday, upon my asking, 'What have you to say to me?' she said, 'Nay, nothing but what you know already: God is love.' I asked, 'Have you any particular promise?' She replied, 'I do not seem to want any: I can live without. I shall die a lump of deformity, but shall meet you all-glorious: and, meantime, I shall still have fellowship with your spirit.'

"(5) Mr. M. asked what she thought the most excellent way to walk in, and what were its chief hindrances. She answered, 'The greatest hindrance is generally from the natural constitution. It was mine to be reserved, to be very quiet, to suffer much, and to say little. Some may think one way more excellent, and some another; but the thing is, to live in the will of God. For some months past, when I have been particularly devoted to this, I have felt such a guidance of His Spirit, and the unction which I have received from the Holy One has so taught me of all things, that I needed not any man should teach me, save as this anointing teacheth.'

"(6) On Friday morning she said, 'I believe I shall die.' She then sat up in her bed, and said, 'Lord, I bless Thee that Thou art ever with me, and all Thou hast is mine. Thy love is greater than my weakness, greater than my helplessness, greater than my unworthiness. Lord, Thou sayest *to corruption, Thou art my sister*! And glory be to Thee, O Jesus, Thou art my Brother. Let me comprehend, with all saints, the length, and breadth, and depth, and height of Thy love! Bless these' (some that were present); 'let them be every moment exercised in all things as Thou wouldst have them to be.'

"(7) Some hours after, it seemed as if the agonies of death were just coming upon her; but her face was full of smiles of triumph, and she clapped her hands for joy. Mrs. C. said, 'My dear, you are more than conqueror through the blood of the Lamb.' She answered, 'Yes, oh yes, sweet Jesus! O death, where is thy sting?' She then lay as in a doze for some time. Afterwards she strove to speak, but could not; however, she testified her love by shaking hands with all in the room.

"(8) Mr. W. then came. She said, 'Sir, I did not know that I should live to see you. But I am glad the Lord has given me this opportunity, and likewise power to speak to you. I love you. You have always preached the strictest doctrine; and I loved to follow it. Do so still, whoever is pleased or displeased.' He asked, 'Do you now believe you are saved from sin?' She said, 'Yes; I have had no doubt of it for many months. That I ever had, was because I did not abide in the faith. I now feel I have kept the faith: and perfect love casteth out all fear. As to you, the Lord promised me, your latter works should exceed your former, though I do not live to see it. I have been a great enthusiast, as they term it, these six months, but never lived so near the heart of Christ in my life. You, sir, desire to comfort the hearts of hundreds by following that simplicity your soul loves.'

"(9) To one who had received the love of God under her prayer, she said, 'I feel I have not followed a cunningly-devised fable; for I am as happy as I can live. Do you press on, and stop not short of the mark.' To Miss M——s she said, 'Love Christ: He loves you. I believe I shall see you at the right hand of God: but *as one star differs from another star in glory, so shall it be in the resurrection.* I charge you, in the presence of God, meet me in that day all glorious within. Avoid all conformity to the world. You are robbed of many of your privileges. I know I shall be found blameless. Do you labour to be found of Him *in peace without spot.*'

"(10) Saturday morning she prayed nearly as follows: 'I know, my Lord, my life is prolonged only to do Thy will. And though I should never eat or drink more' (she had not swallowed anything for near eight-and-twenty hours), 'Thy will be done. I am willing to be kept so for a twelvemonth: *man liveth not by bread alone.* I praise Thee that there is not a shadow of complaining in our streets. In that sense we know not what sickness means. Indeed, Lord, *neither life nor death, nor things present, nor things to come, no, nor any creature, shall separate us from Thy love* one moment. Bless these, that there may be no lack in their souls. I believe there shall not. I pray in faith.'

"On Sunday and Monday she was light-headed, but sensible at times. It then plainly appeared, her heart was still in heaven. One said to her, 'Jesus is our mark.' She replied, 'I have but one mark: I am all spiritual.' Miss M. said to her, 'You dwell in God.' She answered, 'Altogether.' A person asked her, 'Do you love me?' She said, 'Oh, I love Christ; I love my Christ.' To another she said, 'I shall not long be here: Jesus is precious, very precious indeed.' She said to Miss M., 'The Lord is very good! He keeps my soul above all.' For fifteen hours before she died she was in strong convulsions: her sufferings were extreme. One said, 'You are made perfect through sufferings.' She said, 'More and more so.' After lying quiet some time, she said, 'Lord, Thou art strong!' Then, pausing a considerable space, she uttered her last words, 'My Jesus is all in all to me: glory be to Him through time and eternity.' After this she lay still for about half an hour, and then expired without a sigh or groan."

25. The next year, the number of those who believed they were saved from sin still increasing, I judged it needful to

publish, chiefly for their use, *Farther Thoughts on Christian Perfection* :—

"QUESTION 1. How is 'Christ the end of the law for righteousness to every one that believeth'? (Rom. x. 4).

"ANSWER. In order to understand this, you must understand what law is here spoken of; and this, I apprehend, is—(1) The Mosaic law, the whole Mosaic dispensation; which St. Paul continually speaks of as one, though containing three parts, the political, moral, and ceremonial. (2) The Adamic law, that given to Adam in innocence, properly called 'the law of works.' This is in substance the same with the angelic law, being common to angels and men. It required that man should use, to the glory of God, all the powers with which he was created. Now, he was created free from any defect, either in his understanding or his affections. His body was then no clog to the mind; it did not hinder his apprehending all things clearly, judging truly concerning them, and reasoning justly, if he reasoned at all. I say, *if he reasoned*; for possibly he did not. Perhaps he had no need of reasoning till his corruptible body pressed down the mind, and impaired its native faculties. Perhaps, till then, the mind saw every truth that offered as directly as the eye now sees the light.

"Consequently, this law, proportioned to his original powers, required that he should alway think, always speak, and always act precisely right, in every point whatever. He was well able so to do; and God could not but require the service he was able to pay.

"But Adam fell; and his incorruptible body became corruptible; and ever since it is a clog to the soul, and hinders its operations. Hence, at present, no child of man can at all times apprehend clearly, or judge truly. And where either the judgment or apprehension is wrong, it is impossible to reason justly. Therefore, it is as natural for a man to mistake as to breathe; and he can no more live without the one than without the other. Consequently, no man is able to perform the service which the Adamic law requires.

"And no man is obliged to perform it: God does not require it of any man; for Christ is the end of the Adamic as well as the Mosaic law. By His death, He hath put an end to both: He hath abolished both the one and the other with regard to man; and the obligation to observe either the one or the other is vanished away. Nor is any man living bound to observe the Adamic more than the Mosaic law.[1]

"In the room of this, Christ hath established another, namely, the law of faith. Not every one that doeth, but every one that believeth, now receiveth righteousness, in the full sense of the word; that is, he is justified, sanctified, and glorified.

"Q. 2. Are we then dead to the law?

"A. We are 'dead to the law by the

[1] I mean, it is not the condition either of present or future salvation.

body of Christ' given for us (Rom. vii. 4); to the Adamic as well as Mosaic law. We are wholly freed therefrom by His death; that law expiring with Him.

"Q. 3. How, then, are we 'not without law to God, but under the law to Christ'? (1 Cor. ix. 21).

"A. We are without that law; but it does not follow that we are without any law; for God has established another law in its place, even the law of faith: and we are all under this law to God and to Christ: both our Creator and our Redeemer require us to observe it.

"Q. 4. Is love the fulfilling of this law?

"A. Unquestionably it is. The whole law under which we now are is fulfilled by love (Rom. xiii. 8, 10). Faith working or animated by love is all that God now requires of man. He has substituted (not sincerity, but) love, in the room of angelic perfection.

"Q. 5. How is 'love the end of the commandment'? (1 Tim. i. 5).

"A. It is the end of every commandment of God. It is the point aimed at by the whole and every part of the Christian institution. The foundation is faith, purifying the heart; the end, love, preserving a good conscience.

"Q. 6. What love is this?

"A. The loving the Lord our God with all our heart, mind, soul, and strength; and the loving our neighbour, every man, as ourselves, as our own souls.

"Q. 7. What are the fruits or properties of this love?

"A. St. Paul informs us at large: 'Love is long-suffering.' It suffers all the weaknesses of the children of God, all the wickedness of the children of the world; and that not for a little time only, but as long as God pleases. In all, it sees the hand of God, and willingly submits thereto. Meantime, it is 'kind.' In all, and after all, it suffers, it is soft, mild, tender, benign. 'Love envieth not'; it excludes every kind and degree of envy out of the heart. 'Love acteth not rashly,' in a violent, headstrong manner; nor passes any rash or severe judgment. It 'doth not behave itself indecently'; is not rude, does not act out of character. 'Seeketh not her own' ease, pleasure, honour, or profit. 'Is not provoked'; expels all anger from the heart. 'Thinketh no evil'; casteth out all jealousy, suspiciousness, and readiness to believe evil. 'Rejoiceth not in iniquity'; yea, weeps at the sin or folly of its bitterest enemies. 'But rejoiceth in the truth'; in the holiness and happiness of every child of man. 'Love covereth all things,' speaks evil of no man; 'believeth all things' that tend to the advantage of another's character. It 'hopeth all things,' whatever may extenuate the faults which cannot be denied; and it 'endureth all things' which God can permit, or men and devils inflict. This is the 'law of Christ, the perfect law, the law of liberty.'

"And this distinction between the 'law of faith' (or love) and 'the law of works' is neither a subtle nor an unnecessary distinction. It is plain, easy, and intelligible to any common understanding. And it is absolutely necessary, to prevent a thousand doubts and fears, even in those who do walk in love.

"Q. 8. But do we not 'in many things offend all,' yea, the best of us, even against this law?

"A. In one sense we do not, while all our tempers, and thoughts, and words, and works spring from love. But in another we do, and shall do, more or less, as long as we remain in the body. For neither love, nor the 'unction of the Holy One,' makes us infallible: therefore, through unavoidable defect of understanding, we cannot but mistake in many things. And these mistakes will frequently occasion something wrong, both in our temper, and words, and actions. From mistaking his character, we may love a person less than he really deserves. And by the same mistake, we are unavoidably led to speak or act, with regard to that person, in such a manner as is contrary to this law, in some or other of the preceding instances.

"Q. 9. Do we not then need Christ, even on this account?

"A. The holiest of men still need Christ as their Prophet, as 'the light of the world.' For He does not give them light but from moment to moment: the instant He withdraws, all is darkness. They still need Christ as their King; for God does not give them a stock of holiness. But unless they receive a supply every moment, nothing but unholiness would remain. They still need Christ as their Priest, to make atonement for their holy things. Even perfect holiness is acceptable to God only through Jesus Christ.

"Q. 10. May not, then, the very best of men adopt the dying martyr's confession: 'I am in myself nothing but sin, darkness, hell; but Thou art my light, my holiness, my heaven'?

"A. Not exactly. But the best of men may say, 'Thou art my light, my holiness, my heaven. Through my union with Thee, I am full of light, of holiness, and happiness. But if I were left to myself, I should be nothing but sin, darkness, hell.'

"But to proceed: the best of men need Christ as their Priest, their Atonement, their Advocate with the Father; not only as the continuance of their every blessing depends on His death and intercession, but on account of their coming short of the law of love. For every man living does so. You who feel all love, compare yourselves with the preceding description. Weigh yourselves in this balance, and see if you are not wanting in many particulars.

"Q. 11. But if all this be consistent with Christian perfection, that perfection is not freedom from all sin: seeing 'sin is the transgression of the law'; and the perfect transgress the very law they are under. Besides, they need the atonement of Christ; and He is the atonement of nothing but sin. Is, then, the term *sinless perfection* proper?

"A. It is not worth disputing about.

But observe in what sense the persons in question need the atonement of Christ. They do not need Him to reconcile them to God afresh; for they are reconciled. They do not need Him to restore the favour of God, but to continue it. He does not procure pardon for them anew, but 'ever liveth to make intercession for them'; and 'by one offering He hath perfected for ever them that are sanctified' (Heb. x. 14).

"For want of duly considering this, some deny that they need the atonement of Christ. Indeed, exceeding few: I do not remember to have found five of them in England. Of the two, I would sooner give up perfection; but we need not give up either one or the other. The perfection I hold, 'Love rejoicing evermore, praying without ceasing, and in everything giving thanks,' is well consistent with it: if any hold a perfection which is not, they must look to it.

"Q. 12. Does, then, Christian perfection imply any more than sincerity?

"A. Not if you mean by that word, love filling the heart, expelling pride, anger, desire, self-will; rejoicing evermore, praying without ceasing, and in everything giving thanks. But I doubt few use sincerity in this sense. Therefore, I think the old word is best.

"A person may be sincere who has all his natural tempers—pride, anger, lust, self-will. But he is not perfect till his heart is cleansed from these, and all its other corruptions.

"To clear this point a little farther: I know many that love God with all their heart. He is their one desire, their one delight, and they are continually happy in Him. They love their neighbour as themselves. They feel as sincere, fervent, constant a desire for the happiness of every man, good or bad, friend or enemy, as for their own. They rejoice evermore, pray without ceasing, and in everything give thanks. Their souls are continually streaming up to God, in holy joy, prayer, and praise. This is a point of fact; and this is plain, sound, scriptural experience.

"But even these souls dwell in a shattered body, and are so pressed down thereby, that they cannot always exert themselves as they would, by thinking, speaking, and acting precisely right. For want of better bodily organs, they must at times think, speak, or act wrong; not indeed through a defect of love, but through a defect of knowledge. And while this is the case, notwithstanding that defect, and its consequences, they fulfil the law of love.

"Yet as, even in this case, there is not a full conformity to the perfect law, so the most perfect do, on this very account, need the blood of atonement, and may properly for themselves, as well as for their brethren, say, 'Forgive us our trespasses.'

"Q. 13. But if Christ has put an end to that law, what need of any atonement for their transgressing it?

"A. Observe in what sense He has put an end to it, and the difficulty vanishes. Were it not for the abiding merit of His death, and His continual intercession for us, that law would condemn us still. These, therefore, we still need for every transgression of it.

"Q. 14. But can one that is saved from sin be tempted?

"A. Yes; for Christ was tempted.

"Q. 15. However, what you call temptation, I call the corruption of my heart. And how will you distinguish one from the other?

"A. In some cases it is impossible to distinguish, without the direct witness of the Spirit. But in general one may distinguish thus:

"One commends me. Here is a temptation to pride. But instantly my soul is humbled before God; and I feel no pride; of which I am as sure as that pride is not humility.

"A man strikes me. Here is a temptation to anger. But my heart overflows with love. And I feel no anger at all; of which I can be as sure as that love and anger are not the same.

"A woman solicits me. Here is a temptation to lust. But in the instant I shrink back. And I feel no desire or lust at all; of which I can be as sure as that my hand is cold or hot.

"Thus it is, if I am tempted by a present object; and it is just the same if, when it is absent, the devil recalls a commendation, an injury, or a woman, to my mind. In the instant the soul repels the temptation, and remains filled with pure love.

"And the difference is still plainer, when I compare my present state with my past, wherein I felt temptation and corruption too.

"Q. 16. But how do you know that you are sanctified, saved from your inbred corruption?

"A. I can know it no otherwise than I know that I am justified. 'Hereby know we that we are of God,' in either sense 'by the Spirit that He hath given us.'

"We know it by the witness and by the fruit of the Spirit. And, first, by the witness. As, when we were justified, the Spirit bore witness with our spirit that our sins were forgiven; so, when we were sanctified, He bore witness that they were taken away. Indeed, the witness of sanctification is not always clear at first (as neither is that of justification); neither is it afterward always the same, but, like that of justification, sometimes stronger, and sometimes fainter. Yea, and sometimes it is withdrawn. Yet, in general, the latter testimony of the Spirit is both as clear and as steady as the former.

"Q. 17. But what need is there of it, seeing sanctification is a real change, not a relative only, like justification?

"A. But is the new birth a relative change only? Is not this a real change? Therefore, if we need no witness of our sanctification because it is a real change, for the same reason we should need none that we are born of or are the children of God.

"Q. 18. But does not sanctification shine by its own light?

"A. And does not the new birth too? Sometimes it does; and so does sanctification: at others it does not. In the hour of temptation Satan clouds the work of God, and injects various doubts and reasonings, especially in those who have either very weak or very strong understandings. At such times there is absolute need of that witness; without which the work of sanctification not only could not be discerned, but could no longer subsist. Were it not for this, the soul could not then abide in the love of God; much less could it rejoice evermore, and in everything give thanks. In these circumstances, therefore, a direct testimony that we are sanctified is necessary in the highest degree.

"'But I have no witness that I am saved from sin. And yet I have no doubt of it.' Very well: as long as you have no doubt, it is enough; when you have, you will need that witness.

"Q. 19. But what scripture makes mention of any such thing, or gives any reason to expect it?

"A. That scripture, 'We have received, not the spirit that is of the world, but the Spirit which is of God; that we may know the things which are freely given us of God' (1 Corinthians ii. 12).

"Now surely sanctification is one of 'the things which are freely given us of

God.' And no possible reason can be assigned why this should be excepted, when the apostle says, 'We receive the Spirit' for this very end, 'that we may know the things which are' thus 'freely given us.'

"Is not the same thing implied in that well-known scripture, 'The Spirit itself witnesseth with our spirit, that we are the children of God'? (Romans viii. 16). Does He witness this only to those who are children of God in the lowest sense? Nay, but to those also who are such in the highest sense. And does He not witness that they are such in the highest sense? What reason have we to doubt it?

"What if a man were to affirm (as indeed many do) that this witness belongs only to the highest class of Christians? Would not you answer, 'The apostle makes no restriction; therefore, doubtless it belongs to all the children of God'? And will not the same answer hold, if any affirm that it belongs only to the lowest class?

"Consider likewise 1 John v. 19: 'We know that we are of God.' How? 'By the Spirit that He hath given us.' Nay, 'hereby we know that He abideth in us.' And what ground have we, either from Scripture or reason, to exclude the witness, any more than the fruit, of the Spirit, from being here intended? By this then also 'we know that we are of God,' and in what sense we are so; whether we are babes, young men, or fathers, we know in the same manner.

"Not that I affirm that all young men, or even fathers, have this testimony every moment. There may be intermissions of the direct testimony that they are thus born of God; but those intermissions are fewer and shorter as they grow up in Christ; and some have the testimony, both of their justification and sanctification, without any intermission at all; which I presume more might have, did they walk humbly and closely with God.

"Q. 20. May not some of them have a testimony from the Spirit, that they shall not finally fall from God?

"A. They may. And this persuasion, that neither life nor death shall separate them from Him, far from being hurtful, may in some circumstances be extremely useful. These, therefore, we should in nowise grieve, but earnestly encourage them to 'hold the beginning of their confidence steadfast to the end.'

"Q. 21. But have any a testimony from the Spirit that they shall never sin?

"A. We know not what God may vouchsafe to some particular persons; but we do not find any general state described in Scripture, from which a man cannot draw back to sin. If there were any state wherein this was impossible, it would be that of those who are sanctified, who are 'fathers in Christ,' who 'rejoice evermore, pray without ceasing, and in everything give thanks'; but it is not impossible for these to draw back. They who are sanctified, yet may fall and perish (Heb.

x. 29). Even fathers in Christ need that warning: 'Love not the world' (1 John ii. 15). They who 'rejoice, pray,' and 'give thanks without ceasing,' may, nevertheless, 'quench the Spirit' (1 Thess. v. 16, etc.). Nay, even they who are 'sealed unto the day of redemption' may yet 'grieve the Holy Spirit of God' (Eph. iv. 30).

"Although, therefore, God may give such a witness to some particular persons, yet it is not to be expected by Christians in general; there being no scripture whereon to ground such an expectation.

"Q. 22. By what 'fruit of the Spirit' may we 'know that we are of God,' even in the highest sense?

"A. By love, joy, peace, always abiding; by invariable long-suffering, patience, resignation; by gentleness, triumphing over all provocation; by goodness, mildness, sweetness, tenderness of spirit; by fidelity, simplicity, godly sincerity; by meekness, calmness, evenness of spirit; by temperance, not only in food and sleep, but in all things natural and spiritual.

"Q. 23. But what great matter is there in this? Have we not all this when we are justified?

"A. What! total resignation to the will of God, without any mixture of self-will? gentleness, without any touch of anger, even the moment we are provoked? love to God, without the least love to the creature, but in and for God, excluding all pride? love to man, excluding all envy, all jealousy and rash judging? meekness, keeping the whole soul inviolably calm? and temperance in all things? Deny that any ever came up to this, if you please; but do not say, all who are justified do.

"Q. 24. But some who are newly justified do. What, then, will you say to these?

"A. If they really do, I will say they are sanctified; saved from sin in that moment; and that they never need lose what God has given, or feel sin any more.

"But certainly this is an exempt case. It is otherwise with the generality of those that are justified: they feel in themselves more or less pride, anger, and self-will, a heart bent to backsliding. And, till they have gradually mortified these, they are not fully renewed in love.

"Q. 25. But is not this the case of all that are justified? Do they not gradually die to sin and grow in grace, till, at or perhaps a little before death, God perfects them in love?

"A. I believe this is the case of most, but not all. God usually gives a considerable time for men to receive light, to grow in grace, to do and suffer His will, before they are either justified or sanctified; but He does not invariably adhere to this; sometimes He 'cuts short His work': He does the work of many years in a few weeks; perhaps in a week, a day, an hour. He justifies or sanctifies both those who have done or suffered nothing, and who have not had time for a gradual growth either in light or grace. And 'may He not do what He will with' His own? Is thine eye evil, because He is good?'

"It need not, therefore, be affirmed over and over, and proved by forty texts of Scripture, either that most men are perfected in love at last, that there is a gradual work of God in the soul, or that, generally speaking, it is a long time, even many years, before sin is destroyed. All this we know: but we know likewise, that God may, with man's good leave, 'cut short His work,' in whatever degree He pleases, and do the usual work of many years in a moment. He does so in many instances; and yet there is a gradual work, both before and after that moment, so that one may affirm the work is gradual, another it is instantaneous, without any manner of contradiction.

"Q. 26. Does St. Paul mean any more by being 'sealed with the Spirit,' than being 'renewed in love'?

"A. Perhaps in one place (2 Cor. i. 22) he does not mean so much; but in another (Eph. i. 13) he seems to include both the fruit and the witness; and that in a higher degree than we experience even when we are first 'renewed in love.' God 'sealeth us with the Spirit of promise,' by giving us 'the full assurance of hope'; such a confidence of receiving all the promises of God, as excludes the possibility of doubting; with that Holy Spirit, by universal holiness, stamping the whole image of God on our hearts.

"Q. 27. But how can those who

are thus sealed, 'grieve the Holy Spirit of God'?

"A. St. Paul tells you very particularly—(1) By such conversation as is not profitable, not to the use of edifying, not apt to minister grace to the hearers. (2) By relapsing into bitterness, or want of kindness. (3) By wrath, lasting displeasure, or want of tender-heartedness. (4) By anger, however soon it is over; want of instantly forgiving one another. (5) By clamour or bawling, loud, harsh, rough speaking. (6) By evil-speaking, whispering, tale-bearing; needlessly mentioning the fault of an absent person, though in ever so soft a manner.

"Q. 28. What do you think of those in London, who seem to have been lately 'renewed in love'?

"A. There is something very peculiar in the experience of the greater part of them. One would expect that a believer should first be filled with love, and thereby emptied of sin; whereas these were emptied of sin first, and then filled with love. Perhaps it pleased God to work in this manner, to make His work more plain and undeniable; and to distinguish it more clearly from that overflowing love which is often felt even in a justified state.

"It seems likewise most agreeable to the great promise: 'From all your filthiness I will cleanse you; a new heart also will I give you, and a new spirit will I put within you" (Ezek. xxxvi. 25, 26).

"But I do not think of them all alike: there is a wide difference between some of them and others. I think most of them with whom I have spoken, have much faith, love, joy, and peace. Some of these, I believe, are renewed in love, and have the direct witness of it; and they manifest the fruit above described, in all their words and actions. Now, let any man call this what he will, it is what I call perfection.

"But some who have much love, peace, and joy, yet have got the direct witness; and others who think they have, are, nevertheless, manifestly wanting in the fruit. How many, I will not say—perhaps one in ten; perhaps more or fewer. But some are undeniably wanting in long-suffering, Christian resignation. They do not see the hand of God in whatever occurs, and cheerfully embrace it. They do not in everything give thanks, and rejoice evermore. They are not happy; at least not always happy; for sometimes they complain. They say this or that is hard.

"Some are wanting in gentleness. They resist evil, instead of turning the other cheek. They do not receive reproach with gentleness; no, nor even reproof. Nay, they are not able to bear contradiction without the appearance, at least, of resentment. If they are reproved or contradicted though mildly, they do not take it well; they behave with more distance and reserve than they did before. If they are reproved or contradicted harshly, they answer it with harshness; with a loud voice, or with an angry tone, or in a sharp and surly manner. They speak sharply or roughly when they reprove others; and behave roughly to their inferiors.

"Some are wanting in goodness. They are not kind, mild, sweet, amiable, soft, and loving at all times, in their spirit, in their words, in their look and air, in the whole tenor of their behaviour; and that to all, high and low, rich and poor, without respect of persons; particularly to them that are out of the way, to opposers, and to those of their own household. They do not long, study, endeavour by every means, to make all about them happy. They can see them uneasy, and not be concerned; perhaps they make them so; and then wipe their mouths, and say, 'Why, they deserve it; it is their own fault.'

"Some are wanting in fidelity; a nice regard to truth, simplicity, and godly sincerity. Their love is hardly without dissimulation; something like guile is found in their mouth. To avoid roughness, they lean to the other extreme. They are smooth to an excess, so as scarce to avoid a degree of fawning, or of seeming to mean what they do not.

"Some are wanting in meekness, quietness of spirit, composure, evenness of temper. They are up and down, sometimes high, sometimes low; their mind is not well balanced. Their affections are either not in due proportion—they have too much of one, too little of another; or they are not duly mixed and tempered together, so as to counterpoise each other. Hence there is often a jar. Their soul is out of tune, and cannot make the true harmony.

"Some are wanting in temperance. They do not steadily use that kind and degree of food which they know, or might know, would most conduce to the health, strength, and vigour of the body: or they are not temperate in sleep; they do not rigorously adhere to what is best both for body and mind; otherwise they would constantly go to bed and rise early, and at a fixed hour: or they sup late, which is neither good for body nor soul: or they use neither fasting nor abstinence: or they prefer (which are so many sorts of intemperance) that preaching, reading, or conversation, which gives them transient joy and comfort, before that which brings godly sorrow, or instruction in righteousness. Such joy is not sanctified; it doth not tend to, and terminate in, the crucifixion of the heart. Such faith doth not centre in God, but rather in itself.

"So far all is plain. I believe you have faith, and love, and joy, and peace. Yet, you who are particularly concerned know each for yourself that you are wanting in the respects above mentioned. You are wanting either in long-suffering, gentleness, or goodness; either in fidelity, meekness, or temperance. Let us not then, on either hand, fight about words. In the thing we clearly agree.

"You have not what I call perfection: if others will call it so, they may. However, hold fast what you have, and earnestly pray for what you have not.

"Q. 29. Can those who are perfect grow in grace?

"A. Undoubtedly they can; and that not only while they are in the body, but to all eternity.

"Q. 30. Can they fall from it?

"A. I am well assured they can: matter of fact puts this beyond dispute. Formerly we thought, one saved from sin could not fall; now we know the contrary. We are surrounded with instances of those who lately experienced all that I mean by perfection. They had both the fruit of the Spirit, and the witness; but they have now lost both. Neither does any one stand by virtue of anything that is implied in the nature of the state. There is no such height or strength of holiness as it is impossible to fall from. If there be any that cannot fall, this wholly depends on the promise of God.

"Q. 31. Can those who fall from this state recover it?

"A. Why not? We have many instances of this also. Nay, it is an exceeding common thing for persons to lose it more than once, before they are established therein.

"It is therefore to guard them who are saved from sin, from every occasion of stumbling, that I give the following advices. But first I shall speak plainly concerning the work itself.

"I esteem this late work to be of God; probably the greatest now upon earth. Yet, like all others, this also is mixed with much human frailty. But these weaknesses are far less than might have been expected; and ought to have been joyfully borne by all that loved and followed after righteousness. That there have been a few weak, warm-headed men, is no reproach to the work itself; no just ground for accusing a multitude of sober-minded men, who are patterns of strict holiness. Yet (just the contrary to what ought to have been) the opposition is great; the helps few. Hereby many are hindered from seeking faith and holiness by the false zeal of others; and some who at first began to run well are turned out of the way.

"Q. 32. What is the first advice[1] that you would give them?

"A. Watch and pray continually against pride. If God has cast it out, see that it enter no more: it is full as dangerous as desire, and you may slide back into it unawares; especially if you think there is no

---

[1] The advices which follow were published in a separate tract in the year 1762, under the title of "Cautions and Directions given to the greatest Professors in the Methodist Societies," with the following motto:—

"Set the false witnesses aside,
Yet hold the truth for ever fast."

It was evidently intended to guard the people against the mischievous extravagances of George Bell and his friends, a particular account of whom is given in Mr. Wesley's Journal about that period.—EDIT.

danger of it. 'Nay, but I ascribe all I have to God.' So you may, and be proud nevertheless. For it was pride, not only to ascribe anything we have to ourselves, but to think we have what we really have not. Mr. Law, for instance, ascribed all the light he had to God, and so far he was humble: but then he thought he had more light than any man living; and this was palpable pride. So you ascribe all the knowledge you have to God, and in this respect you are humble. But if you think you have more than you really have, or if you think you are so taught of God as no longer to need man's teaching, pride lieth at the door. Yes, you have need to be taught, not only by Mr. Morgan, by one another, by Mr. Maxfield, or me, but by the weakest preacher in London; yea, by all men. For God sendeth by whom He will send.

"Do not therefore say to any who would advise or reprove you, 'You are blind; you cannot teach me.' Do not say, 'This is your wisdom, your carnal reason'; but calmly weigh the thing before God.

"Always remember, much grace does not always imply much light. These do not always go together. As there may be much light where there is but little love, so there may be much love where there is little light. The heart has more heat than the eye; yet it cannot see, and God has wisely tempered the members of the body together, that none may say to another, 'I have no need of thee.'

"To imagine none can teach you but those who are themselves saved from sin, is a very great and dangerous mistake. Give not place to it for a moment: it would lead you into a thousand other mistakes, and that irrecoverably. No; dominion is not founded in grace, as the madman of the last age talked. Obey and regard 'them that are over you in the Lord,' and do not think you know better than them. Know their place and your own; always remembering, much love does not imply much light.

"The not observing this has led some into many mistakes, and into the appearance at least of pride. Oh, beware of the appearance and the thing! Let there 'be in you that lowly mind which was in Christ Jesus.' And 'be ye likewise clothed with humility.' Let it not only fill, but cover you all over. Let modesty and self-diffidence appear in all your words and actions. Let all you speak and do, show that you are little, and base, and mean, and vile in your own eyes.

"As one instance of this, be always ready to own any fault you have been in. If you have at any time thought, spoken, or acted wrong, be not backward to acknowledge it. Never dream that this will hurt the cause of God; no, it will further it. Be therefore open and frank when you are taxed with anything; do not seek either to evade or disguise it; but let it appear just as it is, and you will thereby not hinder but adorn the Gospel.

"Q. 33. What is the second advice which you would give them?

"A. Beware of that daughter of pride, enthusiasm. Oh, keep at the utmost distance from it! Give no place to a heated imagination. Do not hastily ascribe things to God. Do not easily suppose dreams, voices, impressions, visions, or revelations to be from God. They may be from Him. They may be from nature. They may be from the devil. Therefore 'believe not every spirit, but try the spirits whether they be of God.' Try all things by the written word, and let all bow down before it. You are in danger of enthusiasm every hour, if you depart ever so little from Scripture; yea, or from the plain, literal meaning of any text, taken in connection with the context; and so you are, if you despise, or lightly esteem, reason, knowledge, or human learning; every one of which is an excellent gift of God, and may serve the noblest purposes.

"I advise you never to use the words wisdom, reason, or knowledge, by way of reproach. On the contrary, pray that you yourself may abound in them more and more. If you mean worldly wisdom, useless knowledge, false reasoning, say so; and throw away the chaff but not the wheat.

"One general inlet to enthusiasm is expecting the end without the means; the expecting knowledge, for instance, without searching the Scriptures, and consulting the children of God; the expecting spiritual strength, without constant prayer and steady watchfulness; the expecting any blessing without hearing the word of God at every opportunity.

"Some have been ignorant of this device of Satan. They have left off searching the Scriptures. They said, 'God writes all the Scriptures on my heart. Therefore, I have no need to read it.' Others thought they had not so much need of hearing, and so grew slack in attending the morning preaching. Oh, take warning, you who are concerned herein! You have listened to the voice of a stranger. Fly back to Christ, and keep in the good old way, which was 'once delivered to the saints'; the way that even a heathen bore testimony of: 'that the Christians rose early every day to sing hymns to Christ as God.'

"The very desire of 'growing in grace' may sometimes be an inlet of enthusiasm. As it continually leads us to seek new grace, it may lead us unawares to seek something else new, beside new degrees of love to God and man. So it has led some to seek and fancy they had received gifts of a new kind, after a new heart; as—(1) The loving God with all our mind; (2) with all our soul; (3) with all our strength; (4) oneness with God; (5) oneness with Christ; (6) having our life hid with Christ in God; (7) being dead with Christ; (8) rising with Him; (9) the sitting with Him in heavenly places; (10) the being taken up into His throne; (11) the being in the New Jerusalem;

(12) the seeing the tabernacle of God come down among men; (13) the being dead to all works; (14) the not being liable to death, pain, or grief, or temptation.

"One ground of many of these mistakes is, the taking every fresh, strong application of any of these scriptures to the heart, to be a gift of a new kind; not knowing that several of these scriptures are not fulfilled yet; that most of the others are fulfilled when we are justified; the rest the moment we are sanctified. It remains only to experience them in higher degrees. This is all we have to expect.

"Another ground of these, and a thousand mistakes, is, the not considering deeply that love is the highest gift of God—humble, gentle, patient love; that all visions, revelations, manifestations whatever, are little things compared to love; and that all the gifts above mentioned are either the same with or infinitely inferior to it.

"It were well you should be thoroughly sensible of this—the heaven of heavens is love. There is nothing higher in religion—there is, in effect, nothing else; if you look for anything but more love, you are looking wide of the mark, you are getting out of the royal way. And when you are asking others, 'Have you received this or that blessing?' if you mean anything but more love, you mean wrong; you are leading them out of the way, and putting them upon a false scent. Settle it then in your heart, that from the moment God has saved you from all sin, you are to aim at nothing more, but more of that love described in the thirteenth of Corinthians. You can go no higher than this till you are carried into Abraham's bosom.

"I say yet again, beware of enthusiasm. Such is the imagining you have the gift of prophesying, or of discerning of spirits, which I do not believe one of you has; no, nor ever had yet. Beware of judging people to be either right or wrong by your own feelings. This is no scriptural way of judging. Oh, keep close to 'the law and to the testimony!'

"Q. 34. What is the third?

"A. Beware of Antinomianism; 'making void the law,' or any part of it, 'through faith.' Enthusiasm naturally leads to this; indeed they can scarce be separated. This may steal upon you in a thousand forms, so that you cannot be too watchful against it. Take heed of everything, whether in principle or practice, which has any tendency thereto. Even that great truth, that 'Christ is the end of the law,' may betray us into it, if we do not consider that He has adopted every point of the moral law, and grafted it into the law of love. Beware of thinking, 'Because I am filled with love, I need not have so much holiness. Because I pray always, therefore I need no set time for private prayer. Because I watch always, therefore I need no particular self-examination.' Let us 'magnify the law,' the whole written word, 'and make it honourable.'

Let this be our voice: 'I prize Thy commandments above gold or precious stones. Oh, what love have I unto Thy law! all the day long is my study in it.' Beware of Antinomian books; particularly the works of Dr. Crisp and Mr. Saltmarsh. They contain many excellent things; and this makes them the more dangerous. Oh, be warned in time! Do not play with fire. Do not put your hand on the hole of a cockatrice's den. I entreat you, beware of bigotry. Let not your love or beneficence be confined to Methodists, so called, only; much less to that very small part of them who seem to be renewed in love; or to those who believe yours and their report. Oh, make not this your shibboleth! Beware of stillness; ceasing in a wrong sense from your own works. To mention one instance out of many: 'You have received,' says one, 'a great blessing. But you began to talk of it, and to do this and that; so you lost it. You should have been still.'

"Beware of self-indulgence; yea, and making a virtue of it, laughing at self-denial, and taking up the cross daily, at fasting or abstinence. Beware of censoriousness; thinking or calling them that anyways oppose you, whether in judgment or practice, blind, dead, fallen, or 'enemies to the work.' Once more, beware of Solifidianism; crying nothing but, 'Believe, believe!' and condemning those as ignorant or legal who speak in a more scriptural way. At certain seasons, indeed, it may be right to treat of nothing but repentance, or merely of faith, or altogether of holiness; but, in general, our call is to declare the whole counsel of God, and to prophesy according to the analogy of faith. The written word treats of the whole and every particular branch of righteousness, descending to its minutest branches; as, to be sober, courteous, diligent, patient, to honour all men. So, likewise, the Holy Spirit works the same in our hearts, not merely creating desires after holiness in general, but strongly inclining us to every particular grace, leading us to every individual part of 'whatsoever is lovely.' And this with the greatest propriety: for as 'by works faith is made perfect,' so the completing or destroying the work of faith, and enjoying the favour or suffering the displeasure of God, greatly depends on every single act of obedience or disobedience.

"Q. 35. What is the fourth?

"A. Beware of sins of omission; lose no opportunity of doing good in any kind. Be zealous of good works; willingly omit no work, either of piety or mercy. Do all the good you possibly can to the bodies and souls of men. Particularly, 'Thou shalt in any wise reprove thy neighbour, and not suffer sin upon him.' Be active. Give no place to indolence or sloth; give no occasion to say, 'Ye are idle, ye are idle.' Many will say so still; but let your whole spirit and behaviour refute the slander. Be always employed; lose no shred of time; gather up the fragments, that nothing be lost. And whatsoever thy hand findeth to do, do it with thy might. Be 'slow to speak,' and wary in speaking. 'In a multitude of words there wanteth not sin.' Do not talk much; neither long at a time. Few can converse profitably above an hour. Keep at the utmost distance from pious chit-chat, from religious gossiping.

"Q. 36. What is the fifth?

"A. Beware of desiring anything but God. Now you desire nothing else; every other desire is driven out: see that none enter again. 'Keep thyself pure'; let your 'eye' remain 'single, and your whole body shall be full of light.' Admit no desire of pleasing food, or any other pleasure of sense; no desire of pleasing the eye or the imagination, by anything grand, or new, or beautiful; no desire of money, of praise, or esteem; of happiness in any creature. You may bring these desires back; but you need not; you need feel them no more. Oh, stand fast in the liberty wherewith Christ hath made you free!

"Be patterns to all, of denying yourselves, and taking up your cross daily. Let them see that you make no account of any pleasure which does not bring you nearer to God, nor regard any pain which does; that you simply aim at pleasing Him, whether by doing or suffering; that the constant language of your heart, with regard to pleasure or pain, honour or dishonour, riches or poverty, is

'All's alike to me, so I
In my Lord may live and die!'

"Q. 37. What is the sixth?

"A. Beware of schism, of making a rent in the Church of Christ. That inward disunion, the members ceasing to have a reciprocal love 'one for another' (1 Cor. xii. 25), is the very root of all contention, and every outward separation. Beware of everything tending thereto. Beware of a dividing spirit: shun whatever has the least aspect that way. Therefore, say not, 'I am of Paul, or of Apollos'; the very thing which occasioned the schism at Corinth. Say not, 'This is my preacher; the best preacher in England. Give me him, and take all the rest.' All this tends to breed or foment division, to disunite those whom God hath joined. Do not despise or run down any preacher; do not exalt any one above the rest, lest you hurt both him and the cause of God. On the other hand, do not bear hard upon any by reason of some incoherency or inaccuracy of expression; no, nor for some mistakes, were they really such.

"Likewise, if you would avoid schism, observe every rule of the Society and of the bands for conscience' sake. Never omit meeting your class or band; never absent yourself from any public meeting. These are the very sinews of our Society; and whatever weakens, or tends to weaken, our regard for these, or our exactness in attending them, strikes at the very root of our community. As one saith, 'That part of our economy, the private weekly meetings for prayer, examination, and particular exhortation, has been the greatest means of deepening and confirming every blessing that was received by the word preached, and of diffusing it to others who could not attend the public ministry; whereas, without this religious connection and intercourse, the most ardent attempts by mere preaching have proved of no lasting use.'

"Suffer not one thought of separating from your brethren, whether their opinions agree with yours or not. Do not dream that any man sins in not believing you, in not taking your word; or that this or that opinion is essential to the work, and both must stand or fall together. Beware of impatience of contradiction. Do not condemn or think hardly of those who cannot see just as you see, or who judge it their duty to contradict you, whether in a great thing or a small. I fear some of us have thought hardly of others, merely because they contradicted what we affirmed. All this tends to division; and by everything of this kind, we are teaching them an evil lesson against ourselves.

"Oh, beware of touchiness, of testiness, not bearing to be spoken to; starting at the least word; and flying from those who do not implicitly receive mine or another's sayings!

"Expect contradiction and opposition, together with crosses of various kinds. Consider the words of St. Paul: 'To you it is given in the behalf of Christ,'—for His sake, as a fruit of His death and intercession for you,—'not only to believe, but also to suffer for His sake' (Phil. i. 29). 'It is given.' God gives you this opposition or reproach; it is a fresh token of His love. And will you disown the Giver, or spurn His gift, and count it a misfortune? Will you not rather say, 'Father, the hour is come that Thou shouldest be glorified; now Thou givest Thy child to suffer something for Thee: do with me according to Thy will'? Know that these things, far from being hindrances to the work of God, or to your soul, unless by your own fault, are not only unavoidable in the course of Providence, but profitable, yea necessary, for you. Therefore, receive them from God (not from chance) with willingness, with thankfulness. Receive them from men with humility, meekness, yieldingness, gentleness, sweetness. Why should not even your outward appearance and manner be soft? Remember the charity of Lady Cutts. It was said of the Roman Emperor Titus, never any one came displeased from him: but it might be said of her, never any one went displeased to her; so secure were all of the kind and favourable reception which they would meet with from her.

"Beware of tempting others to separate from you. Give no offence which can possibly be avoided; see that your practice be in all things suitable to your profession, adorning the doctrine of God our Saviour. Be particularly careful in speaking of yourself: you may not, indeed, deny the work of God; but speak of it, when you are called thereto, in the most inoffensive manner possible. Avoid all magnificent, pompous words: indeed, you need give it no general name; neither perfection, sanctification, the second blessing, nor the having attained. Rather speak of the particulars which God has wrought for you. You may say, 'At such a time I felt a change which I am not able to express; and since that time I have not felt pride, or self-will, or anger, or unbelief, nor anything but a fulness of love to God and to all mankind.' And answer any other plain question that is asked with modesty and simplicity.

"And if any of you should at any time fall from what you now are, if you should again feel pride or unbelief, or any temper from which you are now delivered—do not deny; do not hide, do not disguise it at all, at the peril of your soul. At all events, go to one in whom you can confide, and speak just what you feel. God will enable him to speak a word in season, which shall be health to your soul. And surely He will again lift up your head, and cause the bones that have been broken to rejoice.

"Q. 38. What is the last advice that you would give them?

"A. Be exemplary in all things; particularly in outward things (as in dress), in little things, in the laying out of your money (avoiding every needless expense), in deep, steady seriousness, and in the solidity and usefulness of all your conversation. So shall you be 'a light, shining in a dark place.' So shall you daily 'grow in grace,' till 'an entrance be ministered unto you abundantly unto the everlasting kingdom of our Lord Jesus Christ.'

"Most of the preceding advices are strongly enforced in the following reflections; which I recommend to your deep and frequent consideration, next to the Holy Scriptures:—

"(1) The sea is an excellent figure of the fulness of God, and that of the blessed Spirit. For as the rivers all return into the sea, so the bodies, the souls, and the good works of the righteous return into God, to live there in His eternal repose.

"Although all the graces of God depend on His mere bounty, yet is He pleased generally to attach them to the prayers, the instructions, and the holiness of those with whom we are. By strong though invisible attractions He draws some souls, through their intercourse with others.

"The sympathies formed by grace far surpass those formed by nature.

"The truly devout show that passions as naturally flow from true as from false love; so deeply sensible are they of the goods and evils of those whom they love for God's sake. But this can only be comprehended by those who understand the language of love.

"The bottom of the soul may be in repose even while we are in many outward troubles; just as the bottom of the sea is calm, while the surface is strongly agitated.

"The best helps to growth in grace are the ill usage, the affronts, and the losses which befall us. We should receive them with all thankfulness, as preferable to all others, were it only on this account,—that our will has no part therein.

"The readiest way to escape from our sufferings is, to be willing they should endure as long as God pleases.

"If we suffer persecution and affliction in a right manner, we attain a larger measure of conformity to Christ, by a due improvement of one of these occasions, than we could have done merely by imitating His mercy, in abundance of good works.

"One of the greatest evidences of God's love to those that love Him is, to send them afflictions, with grace to bear them.

"Even in the greatest afflictions, we ought to testify to God, that, in receiving them from His hand, we feel pleasure in the midst of the pain, from being afflicted by Him who loved us, and whom we love.

"The readiest way which God takes to draw a man to Himself is, to afflict him in that he loves most, and with good reason; and to cause this affliction to arise from some good action done with a single eye; because nothing can more clearly show him the emptiness of what is most lovely and desirable in the world.

"(2) True resignation consists in a thorough conformity to the whole will of God, who wills and does all (excepting sin) which comes to pass in the world. In order to this, we have only to embrace all events, good and bad, as His will.

"In the greatest afflictions which can befall the just, either from heaven or earth, they remain immovable in peace, and perfectly submissive to God by an inward, loving regard to Him, uniting in one all the powers of their souls.

"We ought quietly to suffer whatever befalls us; to bear the defects of others and our own, to confess them to God in secret prayer, or with groans which cannot be uttered; but never to speak a sharp or peevish word, nor to murmur or repine; but thoroughly willing that God should treat you in the manner that pleases Him. We are His lambs, and therefore ought to be ready to suffer, even to the death, without complaining.

"We are to bear with those we cannot amend, and to be content with offering them to God. This is true resignation. And since He has borne our infirmities, we may well bear those of each other for His sake.

"To abandon all, to strip one's self of all, in order to seek and to follow Jesus Christ naked to Bethlehem, where He was born; naked to the hall where He was scourged; and naked to Calvary, where He died on the cross, is so great a mercy, that neither the thing, nor the knowledge of it, is given to any, but through faith in the Son of God.

"(3) There is no love of God without patience, and no patience without lowliness and sweetness of spirit.

"Humility and patience are the surest proofs of the increase of love.

"Humility alone unites patience with love; without which it is impossible to draw profit from suffering; or, indeed, to avoid complaint, especially when we think we have no occasion for what men make us suffer.

"True humility is a kind of self-annihilation; and this is the centre of all virtues.

"A soul returned to God ought to be attentive to everything which is said to him, on the head of salvation, with a desire to profit thereby.

"Of the sins which God has pardoned, let nothing remain but a deeper humility in the heart, and a stricter regulation in our words, in our actions, and in our sufferings.

"(4) The bearing men, and suffering evils in meekness and silence, is the sum of a Christian life.

"God is the first object of our love: its next office is, to bear the defects of others. And we should begin the practice of this amidst our own household.

"We should chiefly exercise our love towards them who most shock either our way of thinking, or our temper, or our knowledge, or the desire we have that others should be as virtuous as we wish to be ourselves.

"(5) God hardly gives His Spirit even to those whom He has established in grace, if they do not pray for it on all occasions, not only once, but many times.

"God does nothing but in answer to prayer; and even they who have been converted to God, without praying for it themselves (which is exceeding rare), were not without the prayers of others.

Every new victory which a soul gains is the effect of a new prayer.

"On every occasion of uneasiness we should retire to prayer, that we may give place to the grace and light of God, and then form our resolutions, without being in any pain about what success they may have.

"In the greatest temptations, a single look to Christ, and the barely pronouncing His name, suffices to overcome the wicked one, so it be done with confidence and calmness of spirit.

"God's command to 'pray without ceasing' is founded on the necessity we have of His grace to preserve the life of God in the soul, which can no more subsist one moment without it, than the body can without air.

"Whether we think of or speak to God, whether we act or suffer for Him, all is prayer, when we have no other object than His love, and the desire of pleasing Him.

"All that a Christian does, even in eating and sleeping, is prayer, when it is done in simplicity, according to the order of God, without either adding to or diminishing from it by his own choice.

"Prayer continues in the desire of the heart, though the understanding be employed on outward things.

"In souls filled with love, the desire to please God is a continual prayer.

"As the furious hate which the devil bears us is termed the roaring of a lion, so our vehement love may be termed crying after God.

"God only requires of His adult children that their hearts be truly purified, and that they offer Him continually the wishes and vows that naturally spring from perfect love. For these desires, being the genuine fruits of love, are the most perfect prayers that can spring from it.

"(6) It is scarce conceivable how strait the way is wherein God leads them that follow Him; and how dependent on Him we must be, unless we are wanting in our faithfulness to Him.

"It is hardly credible of how great consequence before God the smallest things are; and what great inconveniences sometimes follow those which appear to be light faults.

"As a very little dust will disorder a clock, and the least sand will obscure our sight, so the least grain of sin which is upon the heart will hinder its right motion towards God.

"We ought to be in the church as the saints are in heaven, and in the house as the holiest men are in the church: doing our work in the house as we pray in the church; worshipping God from the ground of the heart.

"We should be continually labouring to cut off all the useless things that surround us; and God usually retrenches the superfluities of our souls in the same proportion as we do those of our bodies.

"The best means of resisting the devil is, to destroy whatever of the world remains in us, in order to raise for God, upon its ruins, a building all of love. Then shall we begin, in this fleeting life, to love God as we shall love Him in eternity.

"We scarce conceive how easy it is to rob God of His due, in our friendship with the most virtuous persons, until they are torn from us by death. But if this loss produce lasting sorrow, that is a clear proof that we had before two treasures, between which we divided our heart.

"(7) If, after having renounced all, we do not watch incessantly, and beseech God to accompany our vigilance with His, we shall be again entangled and overcome.

"As the most dangerous winds may enter at little openings, so the devil never enters more dangerously than by little unobserved incidents, which seem to be nothing, yet insensibly open the heart to great temptations.

"It is good to renew ourselves, from time to time, by closely examining the state of our souls, as if we had never done it before; for nothing tends more to the full assurance of faith, than to keep ourselves by this means in humility, and the exercise of all good works.

"To continual watchfulness and prayer ought to be added continual employment. For grace flies a vacuum as well as nature; and the devil fills whatever God does not fill.

"There is no faithfulness like that which ought to be between a guide of souls and the person directed by him. They ought continually to regard each other in God, and closely to examine themselves, whether all their thoughts are pure, and all their words directed with Christian discretion. Other affairs are only the things of men; but these are peculiarly the things of God.

"(8) The words of St. Paul, 'No man can call Jesus Lord, but by the Holy Ghost,' show us the necessity of eyeing God in our good works, and even in our minutest thoughts: knowing that none are pleasing to Him but those which He forms in us and with us. From hence we learn that we cannot serve Him, unless He use our tongue, hands and heart, to do by Himself and His Spirit whatever He would have us to do.

"If we were not utterly impotent, our good works would be our own property; whereas now they belong wholly to God, because they proceed from Him and His grace: while raising our works, and making them all divine, He honours Himself in us through them.

"One of the principal rules of religion is, to lose no occasion of serving God. And since He is invisible to our eyes, we are to serve Him in our neighbour: which He receives as if done to Himself in person, standing visibly before us.

"God does not love men that are inconstant, nor good works that are intermitted. Nothing is pleasing to Him but what has a resemblance of His own immutability.

"A constant attention to the work which God entrusts us with is a mark of solid piety.

"Love fasts when it can, and as much as it can. It leads to all the ordinances of God, and employs itself in all the outward works whereof it is capable. It flies, as it were, like Elijah over the plain, to find God upon His holy mountain.

"God is so great, that He communicates greatness to the least thing that is done for His service.

"Happy are they who are sick, yea or lose their life, for having done a good work.

"God frequently conceals the part which His children have in the conversion of other souls. Yet one may boldly say, that person who long groans before Him for the conversion of another, whenever that soul is converted to God, is one of the chief causes of it.

"Charity cannot be practised right, unless, first, we exercise it the moment God gives the occasion; and, secondly, retire the instant after to offer it to God by humble thanksgiving. And this for three reasons—First, to render Him what we have received from Him. The second, to avoid the dangerous temptation which springs from the very goodness of these works. And the third, to unite ourselves to God, in whom the soul expands itself in prayer, with all the graces we have received, and the good works we have done, to draw from Him new strength against the bad effects which these very works may produce in us, if we do not make use of the antidotes which God has ordained against these poisons. The true means to be filled anew with the riches of grace is thus to strip ourselves of it; and without this it is extremely difficult not to grow faint in the practice of good works.

"Good works do not receive their last perfection till they, as it were, lose themselves in God. This is a kind of death to them, resembling that of our bodies, which will not attain their highest life, their immortality, till they lose themselves in the glory of our souls, or rather of God, wherewith they shall be filled. And it is only what they had of earthly and mortal which good works lose by this spiritual death.

"Fire is the symbol of love; and the love of God is the principle and the end of all our good works. But truth surpasses figure; and the fire of divine love has this advantage over material fire, that it can reascend to its source, and raise thither with it all the good works which it produces. And by this means it prevents their being corrupted by pride, vanity, or any evil mixture. But this cannot be done otherwise than by making these good works in a spiritual manner die in God, by a deep gratitude, which plunges the soul in Him as in an abyss, with all that it is, and all the grace and works for which it is indebted to Him; a gratitude whereby the soul seems to empty itself of them, that they may return to their source, as rivers seem willing to empty themselves when they pour themselves with all their waters into the sea.

"When we have received any favour from God, we ought to retire, if not into our closets, into our hearts, and say, 'I come, Lord, to restore to Thee what Thou hast given; and I freely relinquish it, to enter again into my own nothingness. For what is the most perfect creature in heaven or earth in Thy presence, but a void capable of being filled with Thee and by Thee; as the air which is void and dark is capable of being filled with the light of the sun, who withdraws it every day to restore it the next, there being nothing in the air that either appropriates this light or resists it? Oh, give me the same facility of receiving and restoring Thy grace and good works! I say, *Thine*; for I acknowledge the root from which they spring is in Thee, and not in me.'"

26. In the year 1764, upon a review of the whole subject, I wrote down the sum of what I had observed in the following short propositions:—

"(1) There is such a thing as perfection; for it is again and again mentioned in Scripture.

"(2) It is not so early as justification; for justified persons are to 'go on unto perfection' (Heb. vi. 1).

"(3) It is not so late as death; for St. Paul speaks of living men that were perfect (Phil. iii. 15).

"(4) It is not absolute. Absolute perfection belongs not to man, nor to angels, but to God alone.

"(5) It does not make a man infallible;

none is infallible while he remains in the body.

"(6) Is it sinless? It is not worth while to contend for a term. It is 'salvation from sin.'

"(7) It is 'perfect love' (1 John iv. 18). This is the essence of it: its properties, or inseparable fruits, are, rejoicing evermore, praying without ceasing, and in everything giving thanks (1 Thess. v. 16, etc.).

"(8) It is improvable. It is so far from lying in an indivisible point, from being incapable of increase, that one perfected in love may grow in grace far swifter than he did before.

"(9) It is amissible, capable of being lost; of which we have numerous instances. But we were not thoroughly convinced of this till five or six years ago.

"(10) It is constantly both preceded and followed by a gradual work.

"(11) But is it in itself instantaneous or not? In examining this, let us go on step by step.

"An instantaneous change has been wrought in some believers; none can deny this.

"Since that change they enjoy perfect love; they feel this, and this alone; they 'rejoice evermore, pray without ceasing, and in everything give thanks.' Now, this is all that I mean by perfection; therefore, these are witnesses of the perfection which I preach.

"'But in some this change was not instantaneous.' They did not perceive the instant when it was wrought. It is often difficult to perceive the instant when a man dies; yet there is an instant in which life ceases. And if ever sin ceases, there must be a last moment of its existence, and a first moment of our deliverance from it.

"'But if they have this love now, they will lose it.' They may; but they need not. And whether they do or no, they have it now; they now experience what we teach. They now are all love; they now rejoice, pray, and praise without ceasing.

"'However, sin is only suspended in them; it is not destroyed.' Call it which you please. They are all love to-day; and they take no thought for the morrow.

"'But this doctrine has been much abused.' So has that of justification by faith. But that is no reason for giving up either this or any other scriptural doctrine. 'When you wash your child,' as one speaks, 'throw away the water; but do not throw away the child.'

"'But those who think they are saved from sin say they have no need of the merits of Christ.' They say just the contrary. Their language is—

'Every moment, Lord, I want
The merit of Thy death!'

They never before had so deep, so unspeakable a conviction of the need of Christ in all His offices, as they have now.

"Therefore, all our preachers should

make a point of preaching perfection to believers constantly, strongly, and explicitly; and all believers should mind this one thing, and continually agonise for it."

27. I have now done what I proposed. I have given a plain and simple account of the manner wherein I first received the doctrine of perfection, and the sense wherein I received, and wherein I do receive and teach it to this day. I have declared the whole and every part of what I mean by that scriptural expression. I have drawn the picture of it at full length, without either disguise or covering. And I would now ask any impartial person, What is there so frightful therein? Whence is all this outcry, which for these twenty years and upwards has been made throughout the kingdom; as if all Christianity were destroyed, and all religion torn up by the roots? Why is it that the very name of perfection has been cast out of the mouth of Christians; yea, exploded and abhorred, as if it contained the most pernicious heresy? Why have the preachers of it been hooted at, like mad dogs, even by men that fear God; nay, and by some of their own children; some whom they, under God, had begotten through the Gospel? What reason is there for this, or what pretence? Reason, sound reason, there is none; it is impossible there should. But pretences there are, and those in great abundance. Indeed, there is ground to fear that, with some who treat us thus, it is mere pretence;

that it is no more than a copy of their countenance, from the beginning to the end. They wanted, they sought, occasion against me; and here they found what they sought. "This is Mr. Wesley's doctrine! He preaches perfection!" He does: yet this is not his doctrine any more than it is yours, or any one's else, that is a minister of Christ. For it is His doctrine, peculiarly, emphatically His! it is the doctrine of Jesus Christ. Those are His words, not mine : Ἔσεσθε οὖν ὑμεῖς τέλειοι, ὥσπερ ὁ Πατὴρ ὑμῶν ὁ ἐν τοῖς οὐρανοῖς τέλειός ἐστι,—"Ye shall therefore be perfect as your Father who is in heaven is perfect." And who says ye shall not; or, at least, not till your soul is separated from the body? It is the doctrine of St. Paul, the doctrine of St. James, of St. Peter, and St. John; and no otherwise Mr. Wesley's than as it is the doctrine of every one who preaches the pure and the whole gospel. I tell you, as plain as I can speak, where and when I found this. I found it in the oracles of God, in the Old and New Testament; when I read them with no other view or desire but to save my own soul. But whosesoever this doctrine is, I pray you what harm is there in it? Look at it again; survey it on every side, and that with the closest attention. In one view, it is purity of intention, dedicating all the life to God. It is the giving God all our hearts: it is one desire and design ruling all our tempers. It is the devoting, not a part, but all our soul, body, and substance to

God. In another view, it is all the mind which was in Christ, enabling us to walk as Christ walked. It is the circumcision of the heart from all filthiness, all inward as well as outward pollution. It is a renewal of the heart in the whole image of God, the full likeness of Him that created it. In yet another, it is the loving God with all our heart, and our neighbour as ourselves. Now, take it in which of these views you please (for there is no material difference), and this is the whole and sole perfection, as a train of writings proved to a demonstration, which I have believed and taught for these forty years, from the year 1725 to the year 1765.

28. Now, let this perfection appear in its native form, and who can speak one word against it? Will any dare to speak against loving the Lord our God with all our heart, and our neighbour as ourselves? against a renewal of heart, not only in part, but in the whole image of God? Who is he that will open his mouth against being cleansed from all pollution both of flesh and spirit; or against having all the mind that was in Christ, and walking in all things as Christ walked? What man, who calls himself a Christian, has the hardiness to object to the devoting, not a part, but all our soul, body, and substance to God? What serious man would oppose the giving God all our heart, and the having one design ruling all our tempers? I say again, let this perfection appear in its own shape, and who will

fight against it? It must be disguised before it can be opposed. It must be covered with a bear-skin first, or even the wild beasts of the people will scarce be induced to worry it. But whatever these do, let not the children of God any longer fight against the image of God. Let not the members of Christ say anything against having the whole mind that was in Christ. Let not those who are alive to God oppose the dedicating all our life to Him. Why should you who have His love shed abroad in your heart withstand the giving Him all your heart? Does not all that is within you cry out, "Oh, who that loves can love enough?" What pity that those who desire and design to please Him should have any other design or desire! much more, that they should dread, as a fatal delusion, yea abhor, as an abomination to God, the having this one desire and design ruling every temper! Why should devout men be afraid of devoting all their soul, body, and substance to God? Why should those who love Christ count it a damnable error to think we may have all the mind that was in Him? We allow, we contend, that we are justified freely through the righteousness and the blood of Christ. And why are you so hot against us, because we expect likewise to be sanctified wholly through His Spirit? We look for no favour either from the open servants of sin, or from those who have only the form of religion. But how long will you who worship God in spirit, who are "circumcised with the circumcision not made with hands," set your battle in array against those who seek an entire circumcision of heart, who thirst to be cleansed "from all filthiness of flesh and spirit," and to "perfect holiness in the fear of God"? Are we your enemies because we look for a full deliverance from that "carnal mind which is enmity against God"? Nay, we are your brethren, your fellow-labourers in the vineyard of our Lord, your companions in the kingdom and patience of Jesus. Although this we confess (if we are fools therein, yet as fools bear with us), we do expect to love God with all our heart, and our neighbour as ourselves. Yea, we do believe that He will in this world so "cleanse the thoughts of our hearts by the inspiration of His Holy Spirit, that we shall perfectly love Him, and worthily magnify His holy name."

BRIEF THOUGHTS
on
CHRISTIAN PERFECTION

Some thoughts occurred to my mind this morning concerning Christian perfection, and the manner and time of receiving it, which I believe may be useful to set down.

1. By perfection I mean the humble, gentle, patient love of God and our neighbour, ruling our tempers, words, and actions.

I do not include an impossibility of falling from it, either in part or in whole. Therefore, I retract several expressions in our hymns, which partly express, partly imply, such an impossibility.

And I do not contend for the term *sinless*, though I do not object against it.

2. As to the manner. I believe this perfection is always wrought in the soul by a simple act of faith; consequently in an instant. But I believe in a gradual work both preceding and following that instant.

3. As to the time. I believe this instant generally is the instant of death,

the moment before the soul leaves the body. But I believe it may be ten, twenty, or forty years before.

I believe it is usually many years after justification; but that it may be within five years or five months after it, I know no conclusive argument to the contrary.

If it must be many years after justification, I would be glad to know how many. *Pretium quotus arroget annus?*[1]

And how many days or months, or even years, can any one allow to be between perfection and death? How far from justification must it be; and how near to death?

LONDON, *Jan.* 27, 1767.

THE PROMISE OF SANCTIFICATION

(Ezek. xxxvi. 25, etc.)

BY THE REV. CHARLES WESLEY

1 God of all power, and truth, and grace,
  Which shall from age to age endure;
  Whose word, when heaven and earth shall pass,
  Remains and stands for ever sure:

2 Calmly to Thee my soul looks up,
  And waits Thy promises to prove;
  The object of my steadfast hope,
  The seal of Thine eternal love.

---

[1] This quotation from Horace is thus translated by Boscawen—
" How many years give sanction to our lines?"—EDIT.

3 That I Thy mercy may proclaim,
    That all mankind Thy truth may see,
Hallow Thy great and glorious Name
    And perfect holiness in me.

4 Chose from the world, if now I stand
    Adorn'd in righteousness divine;
If, brought unto the promised land,
    I justly call the Saviour mine:

5 Perform the work Thou hast begun,
    My inmost soul to Thee convert:
Love me, for ever love Thine own,
    And sprinkle with Thy blood my heart.

6 Thy sanctifying Spirit pour,
    To quench my thirst and wash me clean;
Now, Father, let the gracious shower
    Descend, and make me pure from sin.

7 Purge me from every sinful blot:
    My idols all be cast aside:
Cleanse me from every evil thought,
    From all the filth of self and pride.

8 Give me a new, a perfect heart,
    From doubt, and fear, and sorrow free;
The mind which was in Christ impart,
    And let my spirit cleave to Thee.

9 O take this heart of stone away!
    (Thy rule it doth not, cannot own);
In me no longer let it stay;
    O take away this heart of stone!

10 The hatred of my carnal mind
    Out of my flesh at once remove;
Give me a tender heart, resigned,
    And pure, and fill'd with faith and love.

11 Within me Thy good Spirit place,
　　Spirit of health, and love, and power;
　Plant in me Thy victorious grace,
　　And sin shall never enter more.

12 Cause me to walk in Christ my way,
　　And I Thy statutes shall fulfil;
　In every point Thy law obey,
　　And perfectly perform Thy will.

13 Hast Thou not said, who canst not lie,
　　That I Thy law shall keep and do?
　Lord, I believe, though men deny:
　　They all are false; but Thou art true.

14 O that I now, from sin released,
　　Thy word might to the utmost prove!
　Enter into the promised rest,
　　The Canaan of Thy perfect love!

15 There let me ever, ever dwell;
　　Be Thou my God, and I will be
　Thy servant: O set to Thy seal!
　　Give me eternal life in Thee.

16 From all remaining filth within
　　Let me in Thee salvation have;
　From actual and from inbred sin
　　My ransom'd soul persist to save.

17 Wash out my old orig'nal stain:
　　Tell me no more it cannot be,
　Demons or men! The Lamb was slain,
　　His blood was all pour'd out for me!

18 Sprinkle it, Jesu, on my heart:
　　One drop of Thy all-cleansing blood
　Shall make my sinfulness depart,
　　And fill me with the life of God.

19 Father, supply my every need;
   Sustain the life Thyself hast given;
Call for the corn, the living bread,
   The manna that comes down from heaven.

20 The gracious fruits of righteousness,
   Thy blessings' unexhausted store,
In me abundantly increase;
   Nor let me ever·hunger more.

21 Let me no more in deep complain,
   "My leanness, O my leanness!" cry;
Alone consumed with pining want,
   Of all my Father's children I!

22 The painful thirst, the fond desire,
   Thy joyous presence shall remove;
While my full soul doth still require
   The whole eternity of love.

23 Holy, and true, and righteous Lord,
   I wait to prove Thy perfect will;
Be mindful of Thy gracious word,
   And stamp me with Thy Spirit's seal!

24 Thy faithful mercies let me find,
   In which Thou causest me to trust;
Give me Thy meek and lowly mind,
   And lay my spirit in the dust.

25 Show me how foul my heart hath been,
   When all renew'd by grace I am;
When Thou hast emptied me of sin,
   Show me the fulness of my shame.

26 Open my faith's interior eye,
   Display Thy glory from above;
And all I am shall sink and die,
   Lost in astonishment and love.

27 Confound, o'erpower me, with Thy grace ;
   I would be by myself abhorr'd :
  (All might, all majesty, all praise,
    All glory be to Christ my Lord !)

28 Now let me gain perfection's height,
   Now let me into nothing fall !
  Be less than nothing in my sight,
    And feel that Christ is all in all.

ENTIRE SANCTIFICATION
ATTAINABLE IN THIS LIFE

II

Mr. FLETCHER'S
PRACTICAL APPLICATION OF THE DOCTRINE TO VARIOUS CLASSES OF CHRISTIANS

    I. To Christian Pharisees
    II. To Antinomians
    III. To Earnest Seekers of
         Entire Sanctification

PRACTICAL APPLICATION

I

TO CHRISTIAN PHARISEES

I ADDRESS you first, ye perfect Christian pharisees, because ye are most ready to profess Christian perfection, though, alas! ye stand at the greatest distance from perfect humility,—the grace which is most essential to the perfect Christian's character; and because the enemies of our doctrine make use of you first, when they endeavour to root it up from the earth.

That ye may know whom I mean by "perfect Christian pharisees," give me leave to show you your own picture in the glass of a plain description. Ye have professedly entered into the fold where Christ's sheep, which are perfected in love, rest all at each other's feet, and at the feet of the Lamb of God. But how have ye entered? by Christ the door? or at the door of presumption? Not by Christ the door; for Christ is meekness and lowliness manifested in the flesh, but ye are still ungentle and fond of praise. When He pours out His soul as a divine prophet, He says, "Learn of Me, for I am meek and lowly in heart: take My yoke upon you, and ye shall find rest unto your souls." But ye overlook this humble door; your proud, gigantic minds are above stooping low enough to follow Him who "made Himself of no reputation," that He might raise us to heavenly honours; and who, to pour just contempt upon human pride, had His first night's lodging in a stable, and spent His last night partly on the cold ground, in a storm of Divine wrath, and partly in an ignominious confinement, exposed to the greatest indignities which Jews and Gentiles could pour upon Him. He rested His infant head upon hay, His dying head upon thorns. A manger was His cradle, and a cross His death-bed. Thirty years He travelled from the sordid stable to the accursed tree, unnoticed by His own peculiar people. In the brightest of His days, poor fishermen, some Galilean women, and a company of shouting children, formed all his retinue. Shepherds were His first attendants, and malefactors His last companions,

His first beatitude was, "Blessed are the poor in spirit"; and the last, "Blessed are ye when men shall revile you, and persecute you, and say all manner of evil against you falsely, for My sake." His first doctrine was, "Repent"; nor was the last unlike to it: "If I have washed your feet, ye ought also to wash one another's feet; for I have given you an example, that ye should do as I have done to you. He that will be first among you, let him be the last of all." Now, far from practising with godly sincerity this last lesson of our humble Lord, ye do not so much as truly relish the first: ye do not delight in, nay ye abhor, penitential poverty of spirit. Your humility is not cordial, and wrought into your nature by grace; but complimental, and woven into your carriage by art. Ye are humble in looks, in gestures, in voice, in dress, in behaviour, so far as external humility helps you to secure the reputation of perfect Christians, at which ye aspire from a motive of pharisaic ambition; but ye continue strangers to the childlike simplicity and unaffected brokenness of Christ's perfect disciples. Ye are the very reverse of the "Israelites in whom there is no guile"; ye resemble the artful Gibeonites, who, for a time, imposed upon Joshua's artless simplicity; your feigned profession of special grace deceives those of God's children who have more of the simplicity of the dove, than of the serpent's wisdom. Ye choose the lowest place, but ye do not love it; if ye cheerfully take it, it is not among your equals, but among your inferiors, because ye think that such a condescending step may raise the credit of your humility, without endangering your superiority. If ye stoop, and go down, it is not because ye see yourselves unworthy of the seat of honour; but because ye hope that people will, by and by, say to you, "Come up higher." Your pharisaic cunning aims at wearing at once the coronet of genuine humility and the crown of self-exalting pride. Ye love to be esteemed of men for your goodness and devotion. Ye want to be admired for your exactness, zeal, and gracious attainments. The pride of the Jewish Pharisees was coarse in comparison of yours; they wore the rough garment, and you wear the silks, of spiritual vanity: and even when ye dye them in the blood of the Lamb, which you extol in word, it is to draw the confidence of humble Christians by your Christian appearance and language, more than to follow the propensity of a new nature, which loves to be clothed with humility, and feels itself in its own centre when it rests in deep poverty of spirit, and sees that God is all in all.

One of the greatest ends of Christ's coming into the world was to empty us of ourselves, and to fill us with humble love; but ye are still full of yourselves, and void of Christ, that is, void of humility incarnate. Ye still aim at some wrong mark, whether it be self-glory, self-interest, self-pleasure, self-party, or self-applause; in a word, one selfish scheme or another, contrary to the pure love of God and of your neighbour, secretly destroys the root of your profession, and may be compared to the unseen worm that ate the root of Jonah's gourd. Ye have a narrow, contracted spirit; ye do not gladly sacrifice your private satisfaction, your interest, your reputation, your prejudices, to the general interest of truth and love, and to the public good of the whole body of Christ. Ye are yet in secret bondage to men, places, and things. Ye do not heartily entertain the wisdom from above, which is "pure, gentle, easy to be entreated, and full of mercy." Nay, ye are above conviction; gross sinners yield to truth before you. Like Jehu, ye are zealous, and ye pretend that it is for the Lord of hosts; but, alas! it is for your opinions, your party, your honour. In a word, ye do not walk in constant, solemn expectation of death and judgment; your will is not broken; your carnal confidence is yet alive; the heavenly Dove does not sit in your breast; self, wrapt up in a cloak of humility, is still set up in your heart, and in secret you serve that cursed idol more than God. Satan, transformed into an angel of light, has artfully led you to the profession of Christian perfection, through a circle of external performances, through glorious forms of doctrine in the letter, and through a fair show of zeal for complete holiness; the Lord, to punish your formality, has, in part, given you up to your delusion; and now ye as much believe yourselves perfect Christians as the Pharisees, in our Lord's days, believed themselves perfect Jews.

Mr. Wesley, in his *Plain Account of Christian Perfection*, has borne his faithful testimony against such witnesses of perfect love as ye are. If ye despise this address, regard his remarks: "Others," says he, "who think they have the direct witness of their being renewed in love, are, nevertheless, manifestly wanting in the fruit: some are undoubtedly wanting in long-suffering,—Christian resignation. They do not see the hand of God in whatever occurs, and cheerfully embrace it. They do not 'in every thing give thanks,' and 'rejoice evermore.' They are not happy, at least not always happy; for sometimes they complain; they say, 'This is hard.' Some are wanting in gentleness; they resist evil, instead of turning the other cheek. They do not receive reproach with gentleness; no, nor even reproof. Nay, they are not able to bear contradiction without the appearance, at least, of resentment: if they are reproved or contradicted, though mildly, they do not take it well; they behave with more distance and reserve than they did before," etc. "Some are wanting in goodness; they are not kind, mild, sweet, amiable, soft, and loving, at all times, in their spirit, in their words, in their look, in their air, in the whole tenor of their behaviour; and that to all, high and low, rich and poor, without respect of persons; particularly to them that are out of the way, to opposers, and to those of their own household: they do not long, study, endeavour by every means, to make all about them happy. Some are wanting in fidelity, — a nice regard to truth, simplicity, and godly sincerity. Their love is hardly without dissimulation; something like guile is found in their mouth. To avoid roughness, they lean to the other extreme; they are smooth to an excess, so as scarce to avoid a degree of fawning. Some are wanting in meekness — quietness of spirit, composure, evenness of temper; they are up and down, sometimes high, sometimes low; their mind is not well balanced. Their affections are either not in due proportion— they have too much of the one, too little of the other; or they are not duly mixed and tempered together, so as to counterpoise each other. Hence there is often a jar; their soul is out of tune, and cannot make the true harmony. Some are wanting in temperance; they do not steadily use that kind and degree of food which they know, or might know, would most conduce to the health, strength, and vigour of the body. Or they are not temperate in sleep; they do not rigorously adhere to what is best for body and mind; they use neither fasting nor abstinence," etc.

I have described your delusion; but who can describe its fatal consequences? Who can tell the mischief it has done, and continues to do? The few sincere perfectionists, and the multitude of captious imperfectionists, have equally found you out. The former are grieved for you; and the latter triumph through you.

When the sincere perfectionists consider the inconsistency of your profession, they are ready to give up their faith in Christ's all-cleansing blood, and their hope of getting a clean heart in this life. They are tempted to follow the multitudes of professors, who sit themselves down in self-imputed righteousness, or in solifidian notions of an ideal perfection in Christ. And it is well if some of them have not already yielded to the temptation, and begun to fight against the hopes, which they once entertained, of loving God with all their heart. It is well if some, through you, have not been led to say, "I once sweetly enjoyed the thought of doing the will of God on earth, as it is done in heaven. Once I hopefully prayed, God would so cleanse my heart, that I might perfectly love Him, and worthily magnify His holy Name, in this world. But now I have renounced my hopes; and I equally abhor the doctrine of evangelical perfection, and that of evangelical worthiness. I have made a firm agreement with sin. It shall dwell in my heart so long as my soul shall dwell in my body. Neither the word nor the Spirit of Christ shall eject it. When I was a young convert, I believed that Christ could really make an end of all moral pollution, cast out the man of sin, and cleanse us from heart sin, as well as from outward iniquity, in this life; but I soon met with unhumbled, self-willed people who boldly stood up for this glorious liberty, and made me question the truth of the doctrine. Nay, in process of time, I found that some of those who most confidently professed to have attained this salvation were farther from the gentleness, simplicity, catholic spirit, and unfeigned humility of Christ, than many believers who had never considered the doctrine of Christian perfection.

These offences striking in with some disappointments which I myself met with, in feebly seeking the pearl of perfect love, made me conclude that it can no more be found than the philosopher's stone, and that they are all either fools or knaves who set believers upon seeking it. And now I everywhere decry the doctrine of perfection as a dangerous delusion. I set people against it wherever I go; and my zeal in this respect has been attended with the greatest success. I have damped the hopes of many perfectionists, and I have proselyted several to the doctrine of Christian imperfection. With them I now quietly wait to be purified from indwelling sin in the article of death, and to be made perfect in another world, not only in duty to my parents, in loyalty to the king, in charity to the poor, and love to my wife; but also in patience towards those who cross my will, and in love to all my enemies."

This absurd speech is, I fear, the language of many hearts, although it does not openly drop from many lips. Thus are you, O ye perfect pharisees, the great instruments, by which the tempter tears away the shield of those unsettled Israelites, who look more at your inconsistencies than they do at the beauty of holiness, the promise of God, the blood of Christ, and the power of the Spirit.

But this is not all: as ye destroy the budding faith of sincere perfectionists, so ye strengthen the unbelief of the solifidians.[1] Through you their prejudices are grown up into a fixed detestation of Christian perfection. Ye have hardened them in their error, and furnished them with plausible arguments to destroy the truth which ye contend for. Did ye never hear their triumphs? "Ha! ha! So would we have it! These are some of the people who stand up for sinless perfection! they are all alike. Did not I tell you that you would find them out to be no better than temporary monsters? What monstrous pride! What touchiness, obstinacy, bigotry, and stoicism characterises them! How do they strain at gnats and swallow camels! I had rather be an open drunkard than a perfectionist. Publicans and harlots shall enter into the kingdom of heaven before them." These are the cutting speeches to which your glaring inconsistency, and the severe prejudices of our opponents, give birth. Is it not deplorable that your tempers should thus drive men to abhor the doctrine which your lips recommend?

And what do you get by thus dispiriting the real friends of Christian perfection, and by furnishing its sworn enemies with such sharp weapons against it? Think ye that the mischief ye do shall not recoil upon yourselves? Is not Christ the same yesterday, to-day, and for ever? If He detested the perfect pharisaism of unhumbled Jews, will He admire the perfect self-righteousness of aspiring Christians?

---

[1] Men who separate faith from good works.

If He formerly "resisted the proud, and gave grace to the humble," what reason have ye to hope that He will submit to your spiritual pride, and reward your religious ostentation with a crown of glory? Ye perhaps cry out against antinomianism, and I commend you for it; but are ye not deeply tainted with the worst sort of antinomianism—that which starches, stiffens, and swells the soul? Ye justly bear your testimony against those who render the law of Christ of none effect to believers, by degrading it into a rule, which they strip of the punitive and remunerative sanctions with which it stands armed in the sacred records. But are ye not doubly guilty, who maintain that this law is still in force as a law, and nevertheless refuse to pay it sincere, internal obedience? For when ye break the first commandment of Christ's evangelical law, by practically discarding penitential "poverty of spirit"; and when ye transgress the "last," by abhorring the "lowest place," by disdaining to "wash each other's feet," and by refusing to "prefer others in honour before yourselves,"—are ye not guilty of breaking all the law, by breaking it in one point, in the capital point of humble love, which runs through all the parts of the law, as vital blood does through all the parts of the body? Oh, how much more dangerous is the case of an unhumbled man, who stiffly walks in robes of self-made perfection, than that of a humble man, who, through prejudice and the force of example, meekly walks in robes of self-imputed righteousness!

Behold, thou callest thyself a perfect Christian, and restest in the evangelical law of Christ, which is commonly called "the gospel"! Thou maketh thy boast of God, and knowest His will, and approvest the things that are more excellent, even the way of Christian perfection, being instructed out of the gospel; and art confident that thou thyself art a guide of the blind, a light of them who are in darkness, an instructor of the foolish, and a teacher of babes, or imperfect believers; having the form of knowledge and of the truth in the gospel. Thou, therefore, who teachest another, teachest thou not thyself? Thou that preachest another should not break the law of Christ, through breaking it dishonourest thou God? For the Name of God is blasphemed through you, among those who seek an occasion to blaspheme it. (See Rom. ii. 17, etc.) And think ye that ye shall escape the righteous judgment of God? Has Christ no woes but for Jewish Pharisees? Oh, be no longer mistaken! Before ye are punished by being here given up to a reprobate mind, and by being hereafter cast into the hell of hypocrites, the outer darkness where there will be more weeping, wailing, and gnashing of teeth than in any other hell; before ye are overtaken by the awful hour of death, and the dreadful day of judgment, practically learn that Christian perfection is the mind which was in

Christ; especially His humble, meek, quiet mind; His gentle, free, loving spirit. Aim at it by sinking into deep self-abhorrence, and not by using, as ye have hitherto done, the empty talk and profession of Christian perfection, as a step to reach the top of spiritual pride.

Mistake me not: I do not blame you for holding the doctrine of Christian perfection, but for wilfully missing the only way which leads to it; I mean, the humble, meek, and loving Jesus, who says, "I am the way, and the door; by Me if any man enter in, he shall be saved into so great salvation. He that entereth not by" this "door into" this "sheepfold, but climbeth up some other way" (and especially he that climbeth by the way of pharisaic formality), "the same is a thief and a robber": he robs Christ of His glory, and pretends to what He has no more right to, than a thief has to your property. Would ye then be right? Do not cast away the doctrine of an evangelically-sinless holiness, but contend more for it with your heart than with your lips. With all your soul press after such a perfection as Christ, St. Paul, and St. John taught and exemplified; — a perfection of meekness and humble love. Earnestly believe all the woes which the gospel denounces against self-righteous pharisees, and all the blessings which it promises to perfect penitents. Drink less into the letter, and more into the spirit. Thirst after the gentle and humble spirit of Christ, till, like a fountain of living water, it spring up to everlasting life in your heart. Ye have climbed to the pharisaic perfection of Saul of Tarsus, when, "touching the righteousness of the law, he was blameless." Would ye now attain the evangelical perfection which he was possessed of, when he said, "Let us, as many as are perfect, be thus minded"? Only follow him through the regeneration; fall to the dust before God; rise conscious of the blindness of your heart, meekly deplore it with penitential shame; and, if you follow the directions laid down in the third address, I doubt not but, dangerous as your case is at present, you will be, like St. Paul, as eminent for Christian perfection as you have hitherto been for pharisaic holiness.

II

TO ANTINOMIANS

I fear that, next to the persons whom I have just addressed, ye hinder the cause of holiness, O ye believers, who have been deluded into doctrinal antinomianism. Permit me, therefore, to address you next; nor suffer prejudice to make you throw away this expostulation before you have granted it a fair perusal.

Ye directly or indirectly plead for the necessary continuance of indwelling sin in your own hearts, and in the hearts of all true Christians; but may I be so bold as to ask, Who gave you leave so to do? And when were ye commissioned to propagate this unholy gospel? Was it at your baptism, when ye were ranked among Christ's soldiers and received the Christian name, in token that ye would "keep God's holy will and commandments all the days of your life"; and that you would "not be ashamed to fight manfully against the world, the flesh, and the devil, unto your life's end"? Are not these three enemies strong enough sufficiently to exercise your patience, and try your warlike skill to the last? Did your sponsors promise for you that you would quarter a fourth enemy, called "indwelling sin," in your very breast, lest ye should not have enemies enough to fight against? On the contrary, were ye not exhorted, "utterly to abolish the whole body of sin"? If so, is it not strange that ye should spend part of your precious time in pleading, under various pretexts, for the preservation of heart sin—a sin this, which gives life, warmth, and vigour to the whole body of sin? And is it not deplorable that, instead of conscientiously fulfilling your baptismal engagements, ye should attack those who desire to fulfil them by "utterly abolishing the whole body of sin"?

But ye are, perhaps, ministers of the Established Church; and, in this case, I ask, When did the bishop send you upon this warfare? was it at your confirmation, in which he bound upon you your solemn obligations to "keep God's holy will and commandments," so as "utterly to abolish the whole body of sin"? Is it probable that he commissioned you to pull down what he confirmed, and to demolish the perfection which he made you vow to attain, and to "walk in all the days of your life"? If the bishop gave you no such commission at your confirmation, did he do it at your ordination, when he said, "Receive authority to preach the word of God"? Is there no difference between the "word of God," which cuts up all sin, root and branch, and the word of Satan, which asserts the propriety of the continuance of heart sin during the term of life? If not; did the bishop do it when he exhorted and charged you, "never to cease your labour, care, and diligence till you have done all that lieth in you, to bring all such as are committed to your charge to that agreement of faith, and that perfectness of age in Christ, that there shall be no place left among you for error in religion, or viciousness in life"; that is, I apprehend, till the truth of the gospel, and the love of the Spirit, have perfectly purified the minds and renewed the hearts of all your hearers?

How can ye, in all your confessions and sacramental offices, renounce sin, the accursed thing which God abhors, and which obedient believers detest; and yet plead for its life, its strength, its constant energy, so long as we are in this world? We could better bear with you, if ye appropriated a hand or a foot, an eye or an ear, to sin during term of life; but who can bear your pleas for the necessary continuance of sin in the heart? Is it not enough that this murderer of Christ and all mankind rambles about the walls of the city? Will ye still insinuate that he must have the citadel to the last, and keep it garrisoned with filthy lusts, base affections, bad tempers, or "diabolanians," who, like prisoners, show themselves at the grate, and, "like snakes, toads, and wild beasts, are the fiercer for being confined"? Who has taught you thus to represent Christ as the keeper and not the destroyer of our corruptions? If believers are truly willing to get rid of sin, but cannot, because Christ has bolted their hearts with an adamantine decree, which prevents sin from being turned out; if He has irrevocably given leave to indwelling sin to quarter for life in every Christian's heart, as the King of France in the last century gave leave to his dragoons to quarter for some months in the houses of the poor oppressed Protestants, who does not see that Christ may be called the protector of indwelling sin, rather than its enemy?

Ye absurdly complain that the doctrine of Christian perfection does not exalt our Saviour, because it represents Him as radically saving His obedient people from their indwelling sin in this life. But are ye not guilty of the very error which ye charge upon us, when ye insinuate that He cannot or will not say to our inbred sins, "Those Mine enemies which will not that I should reign over them, bring hither, and slay them before me"? If a common judge has power to pass sentence of death upon all the robbers and murderers who are properly prosecuted, and if they are hanged and destroyed in a few days, weeks, or months, in consequence of his sentence, how strangely do ye reflect upon Christ, and revive the Agag within us, when ye insinuate that He, the Judge of all, who was "manifested for this" very "purpose, that He might destroy the works of the devil," so far forgets His errand, that He never destroys indwelling sin in one of His willing people, so long as they are in this world; although that sin is the capital and most mischievous "work of the devil"!

Your doctrine of the necessary continuance of indwelling sin in all faithful believers, traduces not only the Son of Man, but also the adorable Trinity. The Father gives His only-begotten Son, His Isaac, to be crucified, that the ram "sin" may be offered up and slain; but you insinuate that the life of that cursed ram is secured by a decree, which allots it the heart of all believers for a safe retreat, and a warm stable, so long as we are in this world. You represent the Son as an almighty Saviour, who offers to "make us free" from sin, and yet appoints that the galling yoke of indwelling sin shall remain tied to, and bound upon, our very hearts for life. Ye describe the Holy Ghost as a sanctifier, who applies Christ's all-cleansing blood to the believer's heart; filling it with the oil of holiness and gladness; and yet ye suppose that our hearts must necessarily remain desperately wicked and full of indwelling sin! Is it right to pour contempt upon Christianity, by charging such inconsistencies upon Father, Son, and Holy Ghost?

It can hardly be expected that those who thus misrepresent their God should do their neighbour justice. Hence the liberty which ye take to fix a blot upon the most holy characters. What have the prophets and apostles done to you, that ye should represent them, not only as men who had "a heart partly evil to the last," but also as advocates for the necessary indwelling of sin in all believers till death? And why do ye so eagerly take your advantage of holy Paul in particular, and catch at a figurative mode of speech, to insinuate that he was a "carnal wretch, sold under sin," even when he expected "a crown of righteousness" at the hand of his "righteous Judge," for having "finished his course" with the "just men made perfect"? Nay, what have we done to you, that ye should endeavour to take from us the greatest comfort we have in fighting against the remains of sin? Why will ye deprive us of the pleasing and purifying hope of taking the Jericho which we encompass, and killing the Goliath whom we attack? And what has indwelling sin done for you, that ye should still plead for the propriety of its continuance in our hearts? Is it not the root of all outward sin, and the spring of all the streams of iniquity, which carry desolation through every part of the globe? If ye hate the fruit, why do ye so eagerly contend for the necessary continuance of the root? And if ye favour godliness (for many of you undoubtedly do), why do you put such a conclusive argument as this into the mouths of the wicked?—"These good men contend for the propriety of indwelling sin, that grace may abound. And why should we not plead for the propriety of outward sin, for the same important reason? Does not God approve of an honest heart, which scorns to cloke inward iniquity with outward demureness"?

A writer lately published an ingenious dialogue, called "A Lash at Enthusiasm," in which he uses an argument against pleading for lukewarmness, which, with very little variation, may be retorted against his pleading for indwelling sin. "Suffer me," says he, "to put the sentiments of such persons" as plead for the middle way of lukewarmness, "into the form of a prayer, which we may suppose would run in some such expressions as the following:—'O Lord, Thy word requires that I should love Thee with all my heart, with all my mind, with all my soul, and with all my strength, that I should renounce the world,'" and indwelling sin, "'and should present myself as a holy, reasonable, and lively sacrifice unto Thee; but, Lord, these are such over-righteous extremes,'" and such heights of sinless perfection, "'as I cannot away with. Therefore grant that Thy love, and a moderate share of the love of the world,'" or of indwelling sin, "'may both reign,'" or at least continue, "'in my heart at once. I ask it for Jesus Christ's sake. Amen.'" Mr. Hill justly adds: "Now, dear madam, if you are shocked at such a petition, consider that it is the exact language of your own heart, whilst you can plead for what you call the 'middle way' of religion." And I beg leave to take up his argument, and to add with equal propriety, "Now, dear sirs, if you are shocked at such a petition, consider that it is the exact language of your own hearts, whilst ye can plead for what ye call 'indwelling sin,' or the remains of sin."

Nor can I see what ye get by such a conduct. The excruciating thorn of indwelling sin sticks in your hearts: we assert that Christ can and will extract it, if ye plead His promise of sanctifying you wholly, in soul, body, and spirit. But ye say, "This cannot be: the thorn must stay in till death extract it; and the leprosy shall cleave to the walls till the house is demolished. Just as if Christ, by radically cleansing the lepers in the days of His flesh, had not given repeated proofs of the absurdity of your argument; just as if part of the gospel was not, "The lepers are cleansed," and, "If the Son make you free, ye shall be free indeed"!

If ye get nothing in pleading for Christian imperfection, permit me to tell you what you lose by it, and what ye might get by steadily going on to perfection.

1. If ye earnestly aimed at Christian perfection, ye would have a bright testimony in your own soul, that you are sincere, and that ye walk agreeably to baptismal engagements. I have already observed, that some of the most pious Calvinists doubt if those who do not pursue Christian perfection are Christians at all. Hence it follows, that the more earnestly you pursue it, the stronger will be your confidence that you are upright Christians. And when ye shall be perfected in love, ye shall have that evidence of your sincerity which will perfectly

"cast out" servile "fear which hath torment," and nourish the filial fear which has safety and delight. It is hard to conceive how we can constantly enjoy the full assurance of faith out of the state of Christian perfection. For, so long as a Christian inwardly breaks Christ's evangelical law, he is justly condemned in his own conscience. If his heart does not condemn him for it, it is merely because he is asleep in the lap of antinomianism. On the other hand, says St. John, "If our heart condemn us, God is greater than our heart, and knoweth all things" that make for our condemnation. But if we "love in deed and in truth," which none but the perfect do at all times, "hereby we know that we are of the truth, and shall assure our hearts before Him" (1 John iii. 18–20).

2. The perfect Christian, who has left all to follow Christ, is peculiarly near and dear to God. He is, if I may use the expression, one of God's favourites; and his prayers are remarkably answered. This will appear to you indubitable, if ye can receive the testimony of those who are perfected in obedient love. "Beloved," say they, "whatsoever we ask, we receive of Him; because we keep His commandments, and do those things which are pleasing in His sight"; that is, because we are perfected in obedient love (1 John iii. 21, 22). This peculiar blessing ye lose by despising Christian perfection. Nay, so great is the union which subsists between God

and the perfect members of His Son, that it is compared to dwelling in God, and having God dwelling in us, in such a manner, that the Father, the Son, and the Comforter are said to "make their abode" with us. "At that day," when ye shall be perfected in one, "ye shall know that I am in My Father, and you in Me, and I in you. If a man love Me, he will keep My words; and My Father will love him; and we will come to him, and make our abode with him" (John xiv. 20, 23). Again: "He that keepeth God's commandments dwelleth in God, and God in him" (1 John iii. 24). "Ye are My" dearest "friends, if ye do whatsoever I command you"; that is, if ye attain the perfection of your dispensation (John xv. 14). Once more: "Keep My commandments, and I will pray the Father, and He shall give you another Comforter, that He may abide with you for ever" (John xiv. 15, 16). From these Scriptures it appears that, under every dispensation, the perfect, or they who keep the commandments, have unspeakable advantages, from which the lovers of imperfection debar themselves.

3. Ye bring far less glory to God, in the state of indwelling sin, than ye would do if ye were perfected in love; for perfect Christians (all things being equal) glorify God more than those who remain full of inbred iniquity. Hence it is, that, in the very chapter where our Lord so strongly presses Christian perfection upon His disciples, He says, "Let your light so

shine before men, that they may see your good works, and glorify your Father who is in heaven" (Matt. v. 16). For, "herein is My Father glorified, that ye bear much fruit" (John xv. 8). It is true that the fruit of the perfect is not always relished by men who judge only according to appearances; but God, who judges righteous judgment, finds it rich and precious; and therefore the two mites which the poor widow gave with a cheerful and perfect heart were more precious in His account, and brought Him more glory, than all the money which the imperfect worshippers cast into the treasury, though some of them "cast in much." Hence also our Lord commanded that the work of perfect love which Mary wrought, when she anointed His feet for His burial, "should be told for a memorial of her wherever this" (the Christian) "gospel should be preached in the whole world." Such is the honour which the Lord puts upon the branches in Him that bear fruit to perfection.

4. The perfect Christian, all things being equal, is a more useful member of society than the imperfect. Never will ye be such humble men, such good parents, such dutiful children, such loving brothers, such loyal subjects, such kind neighbours, such indulgent husbands, and such faithful friends, as when ye shall have obtained the perfect sincerity of obedience. Ye will then, in your degree, have the simplicity of the gentle dove, the patience of the laborious ox, the courage

of the magnanimous lion, and the wisdom of the wary serpent, without any of its poison. In your little sphere of action, ye will abound in the work of faith, the patience of hope, and the labour of love, far more than ye did before; for a field properly weeded, and cleared from briers, is naturally more fruitful than one which is shaded by spreading brambles, or filled with the indwelling roots of noxious weeds; it being a capital mistake of the spiritual husbandmen, who till the Lord's field in mystical Geneva, to suppose that the plant of humility thrives best when the roots of indwelling sins are twisted around its root.

5. None but "just men made perfect" are "meet to be made partakers of the inheritance among the saints in light"; an inheritance this, which no man is fit for till he has "purified himself from all filthiness of the flesh and spirit." If modern divines, therefore, assure you that a believer, full of indwelling sin, has a full title to heaven, believe them not; for the Holy Ghost has said that the believer who "breaks the law" of liberty "in one point, is guilty of all," and that "no defilement shall enter" into heaven. And our Lord Himself has assured us that "the pure in heart shall see God"; and that they who "were ready" for that sight "went in with the bridegroom to the marriage-feast of the Lamb." And who is ready? Undoubtedly, the believer whose lamp is trimmed and burning. But is a spiritual lamp trimmed, when its

flame is darkened by the black fungus of indwelling sin? Again, who shall be saved into glory, but the man whose "heart is washed from iniquity"? But is that heart washed which continues full of indwelling corruption? Woe be, therefore, to the heathens, Jews, and Christians who trifle away the accepted time, and die out of a state of heathen, Jewish, or Christian perfection! They have no chance of going to heaven, but through the purgatory preached by the heathens, the papists, and the Calvinists. And should the notions of these purgatories be groundless, it unavoidably follows that unpurged or imperfect souls must, at death, rank with the unready souls, whom our Lord calls "foolish virgins," and against whom the door of heaven will be shut. How awful is this consideration, my dear brethren! How should it make us stretch every nerve, till we have attained the perfection of our dispensation! I would not encourage tormenting fears in an unscriptural manner; but I should rejoice if all who call Jesus "Lord" would mind His solemn declarations: "I say unto you," My friends, "Be not afraid of them that kill the body," etc.; "but I will forewarn you whom you shall fear: fear Him who, after He hath killed, hath power to cast into hell: yea, I say unto you, Fear Him," who will burn, in the fire of wrath, those who harbour the indwelling man of sin, lest he should be utterly consumed by the fire of love.

Should ye cry out against this doctrine,

and ask if all imperfect Christians are in a damnable state, we reply, that so long as a Christian believer sincerely presses after Christian perfection, he is safe, because he is in the way of duty; and were he to die at midnight, before midnight God would certainly bring him to Christian perfection, or bring Christian perfection to him; for we "are confident of this very thing, that He who hath begun a good work in them will perform it until the day of Jesus Christ," because they "work out their own salvation with fear and trembling." But if a believer falls, loiters, and rests upon former experiences, depending upon a self-made, pharisaical perfection, or upon a self-implied, antinomian perfection, our chief message to him is that of St. Paul: "Awake, thou that sleepest; awake to righteousness, and sin not, for thou hast not the" heart-purifying "knowledge of God, which is eternal life. Arise from the dead"; call for oil, "and Christ will give thee light." Otherwise, thou shalt share the dreadful fate of the lukewarm Laodiceans, and of the foolish virgins, whose "lamps went out," instead of "shining more and more to the perfect day."

6. This is not all. As ye will be fit for judgment, and a glorious heaven, when ye shall be perfected in love, so you will actually enjoy a gracious heaven in your own soul. You will possess within you the kingdom of God, which consists in settled "righteousness, peace, and joy in the Holy Ghost." But, so long as ye neglect Christian perfection, and continue

"sold under" indwelling "sin," ye not only risk the loss of the heaven of heavens, but ye lose a little heaven upon earth; for perfect Christians are so full of peace and love, that they "triumph in Christ with joy unspeakable and full of glory," and "rejoice in tribulation," with a "patience" which "has its perfect work." Yea, they "count it all joy when they fall into divers trials"; and such is their deadness to the world, that they "are exceeding glad, when men say all manner of evil of them falsely for Christ's sake." How desirable is such a state! And who, but the blessed above, can enjoy a happiness superior to that of him who can say, "I am ready to be offered up. The sting of death is sin, and the strength of sin is the law; but, O death, where is thy sting? Not in my heart, since the righteousness of the law is fulfilled in us, who walk not after the flesh, but after the Spirit. Not in my mind, for to be spiritually minded is life and peace." Now, this peculiar happiness ye lose, so long as ye continue imperfect Christians.

7. But, supposing a Christian who dies in a state of Christian imperfection can escape damnation, and make shift to get to heaven, it is certain that he cannot go into the glorious mansion of perfect Christians, nor shine among the stars of the first magnitude. The wish of my soul is, that, if God's wisdom has so ordered it, imperfect Christians may one day rank among perfect Jews, or perfect heathens. But, even upon this supposi-

tion, what will they do with their indwelling sin? For a perfect Gentile and a perfect Jew are "without guile," according to their light, as well as a perfect Christian. Lean not then to the doctrine of the propriety and continuance of indwelling sin till death—a doctrine this, on which a Socrates or a Melchizedek would be afraid to venture his heathen perfection and eternal salvation. On the contrary, by Christian perfection ye may rise to the brightest crown of righteousness, and "shine like the sun in the kingdom of your Father." Oh for a noble ambition to obtain one of the first seats in glory! Oh for a constant, evangelical striving, to have the most "abundant entrance ministered unto you into the kingdom of God!" Oh for a throne among those peculiarly redeemed saints who sing the new song, which none can learn but themselves! It is not Christ's to give those exalted thrones out of mere distinguishing grace. No; they may be forfeited, for they shall be given to those for whom they are prepared; and they are prepared for them who, evangelically speaking, are "worthy." "They shall walk with Me in white, for they are worthy," says Christ; and they shall "sit at My right hand, and at My left, in My kingdom," who shall be worthy of that honour: "for them that honour Me, says the Lord, I will honour." "Behold, I come quickly; My reward is with Me, and I will render to every man according to his works." And what reward, think ye, will Christ give you, O my dear, mistaken brethren, if He finds you still passing jests upon the doctrine of Christian perfection, which He so strongly recommends? still pleading for the continuance of indwelling sin, which He so greatly abhors?

8. Your whole system of indwelling sin and imputed perfection stands upon two of the most dangerous and false maxims which were ever advanced. The first, which begets antinomian presumption, runs thus: "Sin cannot destroy us either in this world or in the world to come"; and the second, which is productive of antinomian despair, is, "Sin cannot be destroyed in this world." Oh, how hard is it for those who worship where these syren songs pass for sweet songs of Sion, not to be drawn into one of these fatal conclusions! "What need is there of attacking sin with so much eagerness since, even in the Name of the Lord, I cannot destroy it? And why should I resist it with so much watchfulness, since my eternal life and salvation are absolutely secured, and the most poisonous cup of iniquity cannot destroy me, though I should drink of it every day for months or years?" If ye fondly think that you can neither go backward into a sinful, cursed Egypt, nor yet go forward into a sinless, holy Canaan, how natural will it be for you to say, "Soul, take thy ease," and rest awhile in this wilderness on the pillow of self-imputed perfection! Oh, how many are surprised by the midnight cry in this Laodicean rest! What numbers meet

death with a solifidian "Lord! Lord!" in their mouths, and with indwelling sin in their hearts! And how inexpressible will be our horror, if we perceive our want of holiness and Christian perfection, only when it will be too late to attain them! To conclude—

9. Indwelling sin is not only the sting of death, but the very hell of hells if I may use the expression; for a sinless saint in a local hell would dwell in a holy, loving God; and, of consequence, in a spiritual heaven: like Shadrach, in Nebuchadnezzar's fiery furnace, he might have devouring flames curling about him; but within him he would still have the flame of divine love, and the joy of a good conscience. But so much of indwelling sin as we carry about us, so much of indwelling hell, so much of the sting which pierces the damned, so much of the spiritual fire which will burn up the wicked, so much of the never-dying worm which will prey upon them, so much of the dreadful instrument which will rack them, so much of Satan's image which will frighten them, so much of the characteristic by which the devil's children shall be distinguished from the children of God, so much of the black mark whereby the goats shall be separated from the sheep. To plead, therefore, for the continuance of indwelling sin, is no better than to plead for keeping in your hearts one of the sharpest stings of death, and one of the hottest coals in hell fire. On the other hand, to attain Christian perfection is to have the last feature of

Belial's image erased from your loving souls, the last bit of the sting of death extracted from your composed breasts, and the last spark of hell fire extinguished in your peaceful bosoms. It is to enter into the spiritual rest which remains on earth for the people of God; a delightful rest this, where your soul will enjoy a calm in the midst of outward storms; and where your spirit will no longer be tossed by the billows of swelling pride, dissatisfied avarice, pining envy, disappointed hopes, fruitless cares, dubious anxiety, turbulent anger, fretting, impatient, and racking unbelief. It is to enjoy that even state of mind, in which all things will work together for your good. There your love will bear its excellent fruits during the sharpest winter of affliction, as well as in the finest summer of prosperity. There you will be more and more settled in peaceful humility; there you will continually grow in a holy familiarity with the Friend of penitent sinners; and your prospect of eternal felicity will brighten every day.

Innumerable are the advantages which established, perfect Christians have over carnal, unsettled believers, who continue sold under indwelling sin. And will ye despise those blessings till your dying day, O ye prejudiced imperfectionists? Will ye secure to yourselves the contrary curses? Nay, will ye entail them upon the generations which are yet unborn, by continuing to print, preach, or argue for the continuance of indwelling sin, the capital woe belonging to the devil and his angels? God forbid! We hope better things from you; not doubting but the error of several of you lies chiefly in your judgment, and springs from a misunderstanding of the question, rather than from a malicious opposition to that holiness without which no man shall see the Lord. With pleasure we remember and follow St. Jude's loving direction: "Of some" (the simple-hearted, who are seduced into antinomianism) "have compassion; making a difference; and others" (the bigots and obstinate seducers, who wilfully shut their eyes against the truth) "save with fear; hating even the garment spotted by the flesh"; although they will not be ashamed to plead for the continuance of a defiling fountain of carnality in the very heart of all God's people. We are fully persuaded, my dear brethren, that we should wrong you if we did not acknowledge that many of you have a sincere desire to be saved by Christ into all purity of heart and life; and with regard to such imperfectionists, our chief complaint is, that their desire is "not according to knowledge."

If others of you of a different stamp should laugh at these pages, and, still producing banter instead of argument, should continue to say, "Where are your perfect Christians? Show us but one, and we will believe your doctrine of perfection," I shall just put them in mind of St. Peter's awful prophecy: "Know this first, that there shall come in the last days scoffers, walking after their own" indwelling "lusts, and saying, Where is the promise of His" spiritual "coming"—"to make an end of sin," "throughly to purge His floor, and to burn the chaff with unquenchable fire?"—"For since the fathers fell asleep, all things continue as they were from the beginning": all believers are still "carnal and sold under sin," as well as father Paul. And if such mockers continue to display their prejudice by such taunts, I shall take the liberty to show them their own picture, by pointing at those prejudiced professors of old who said, concerning the most perfect of all the perfect, "What sign showest Thou," that we may receive Thy doctrine? "Come down from the cross, and we will believe." Oh the folly and danger of such scoffs! "Blessed is he that sitteth not in" this "seat of the scornful," and "maketh much of them that fear the Lord." Yea, he is "blessed" next to them who "are undefiled" (perfect) "in the way, who walk in the law of the Lord, keep His testimonies, and seek Him with their whole heart" (Psalm cxix. 1, 2).

Should ye ask, "To what purpose do you make all this ado about Christian perfection? Do those who maintain this doctrine live more holy and useful lives than other believers?" I answer—

1. Everything being equal, they undoubtedly do, if they hold not the truth in unrighteousness; for the best principles, when they are cordially embraced, will always produce the best practices. But, alas! too many merely contend for Chris-

tian perfection in a speculative, systematical manner. They recommend it to others with their lips, as a point of doctrine which makes a part of their religious system, instead of following after it with their hearts, as a blessing which they must attain, if they will not be found as unprepared for judgment as the foolish virgins. These perfectionists are, so far, hypocrites: nor should their fatal inconsistency make us despise the truth which they contend for, any more than the conduct of thousands, who contend for the truth of the Scriptures, while they live in full opposition to the Scriptures, ought to make us despise the Bible.

2. On the other hand, some gracious persons, like the pious and inconsistent antinomians, speak against Christian perfection with their lips, but cannot help following hard after it with their hearts; and, while they do so, they sometimes attain the thing, although they continue to quarrel with the name. These perfect imperfectionists undoubtedly adorn the gospel of Christ far more than the imperfect, hypocritical perfectionists whom I have just described; and God, who looks at the simplicity of the heart more than at the consistency of the judgment, pities their mistakes, and accepts their works.

But, 3. Some there are who both maintain doctrinally and practically the necessity of a perfect devotedness of ourselves to God. They hold the truth, and they hold it in wisdom and righteousness: their tempers and conduct enforce it, as well as their words and profession; and, on this account, they have a great advantage over the two preceding classes of professors. Reason and revelation jointly crown the orthodoxy and faithfulness of these perfect perfectionists, who neither strengthen the hands of the wicked, nor excite the wonder of the judicious, by absurdly pleading for indwelling sin with their lips while they strive to work righteousness with their hands and hearts. If ye candidly weigh this threefold distinction, I doubt not but ye will blame the irrational inconsistency of holy imperfectionists, condemn the immoral inconsistency of unholy perfectionists, and agree with me, that the most excellent Christian is a consistent, holy perfectionist.

And now, my dear, mistaken brethren, take in good part these plain solutions, expostulations, and reproofs; and give glory to God, by believing that He can and will yet save you to the uttermost from your evil tempers, if ye humbly come to Him by Christ. Day and night ask of Him the new heart which keeps the commandments; and when ye shall have received it, if you keep it with all diligence, sin shall no more pollute it than it polluted our Lord's soul when He said, 'If ye keep My commandments, ye shall abide in My love; even as I have kept My Father's commandments, and abide in His love." Burn, in the meantime, the unhallowed pens, and bridle the rash tongues, with which ye have pleaded for the continuance of sin till death. Honour us with the right hand of fellowship; and, like reconciled brethren, let us, at every opportunity, lovingly fall upon our knees together, to implore the help of Him who "can do far exceeding abundantly above all that we ask or think." Nor let us give Him any rest, till He has perfected all our souls in the charity which "rejoiceth in the truth" without prejudice, in the obedience which keeps the commandments without reserve, and in the perseverance which finds that "in keeping of them there is great reward."

Nothing but such a conduct as this can remove the stumblingblocks which the contentions ye breed have laid in the way of a deistical world. When the men whom your mistakes have hardened will see you listen to Scripture and reason, who knows but their prejudices may subside, and some of them may yet say, "See the good which arises from friendly controversy! See how these Christians desire to be perfected in one! They now understand one another. Babylonish confusion is at an end; evangelical truth prevails; and love, the most delicious fruit of truth, visibly grows to Christian perfection." God grant that, through the concurrence of your candour, this may soon be the language of all those whom the bigotry of professors has confirmed in their prejudices against Christianity.

Should this plain address have so far worked upon you, my dear brethren, as to abate the force of your aversion to the doctrine of pure love, or to stagger your unaccountable faith in a death-purgatory, and should you seriously ask which is the way to Christian perfection, I entreat you to pass on to the next section, where, I hope, you will find a scriptural answer to some important questions which, I trust, a few of you are, by this time, ready to propose.

III

TO EARNEST SEEKERS OF ENTIRE SANCTIFICATION

Your regard for Scripture and reason, and your desire to answer the end of God's predestination by "being conformed to the image of His Son," have happily kept or reclaimed you from antinomianism.

Ye see the absolute necessity of personally "fulfilling the law of Christ"; your bosom glows with desire to "perfect holiness in the fear of God"; and, far from blushing to be called "perfectionists," ye openly assert that a perfect faith, productive of perfect love to God and man, is the pearl of great price, for which you are determined to sell all, and which, next to Christ, you will seek early and late, as the one thing needful for your spiritual and eternal welfare. Some directions, therefore, about the manner of seeking this pearl cannot but be acceptable to you, if they are scriptural and rational; and such, I humbly trust, are those which follow :—

1. First, if ye would attain an evangelically sinless perfection, let your full assent to the truth of that deep doctrine firmly stand upon the evangelical foundation of a precept and a promise. A pre-

cept without a promise would not sufficiently animate you; nor would a promise without a precept properly bind you; but a Divine precept and a Divine promise form an unshaken foundation. Let, then, your faith deliberately rest her right foot upon these precepts:—

"Hear, O Israel: Thou shalt love the Lord thy God with all thine heart, and with all thy soul, and with all thy might" (Deut. vi. 4, 5). "Thou shalt not hate thy neighbour in thy heart: thou shalt in any wise rebuke thy neighbour, and not suffer sin upon him. Thou shalt not avenge, nor bear any grudge against the children of thy people; but thou shalt love thy neighbour as thyself: I am the Lord. Ye shall keep My statutes" (Lev. xix. 17-19). "And now, Israel, what doth the Lord thy God require of thee, but to fear the Lord thy God, to walk in His ways, and to love Him, and to serve the Lord thy God with all thy heart and with all thy soul, to keep the commandments of the Lord thy God, and His statutes, which I command thee this day for thy good," etc. "Circumcise therefore the foreskin of your heart, and be no more stiff-necked" (Deut. x. 12, etc.). "Serve God with a perfect heart and a willing mind; for the Lord searcheth all hearts, and understandeth the imaginations of the thoughts" (1 Chron. xxviii. 9).

Should unbelief suggest that these are only Old Testament injunctions, trample upon the false suggestion, and rest the same foot of your faith upon the following

New Testament precepts: "Think not that I am come to destroy the law, or the prophets." I say unto you, "Love your enemies, bless them that curse you, do good to them that hate you," etc.; "that ye may be the children of your Father who is in heaven," etc. "For if ye love them which love you, what reward have ye? Do not even the publicans the same?" "Be ye therefore perfect, even as your Father which is in heaven is perfect" (Matt. v. 17, 44, etc.). "If thou wilt enter into life, keep the commandments" (Matt. xix. 17). "Bear ye one another's burdens, and so fulfil the law of Christ." (Gal. vi. 2). "This is My commandment, That ye love one another, as I have loved you" (John xv. 12). "He that loveth another hath fulfilled the law. For this, Thou shalt not commit adultery," etc., "Thou shalt not covet; and if there be any other commandment, it is briefly comprehended in this saying, Thou shalt love thy neighbour as thyself. Love worketh no ill," etc.; "therefore love is the fulfilling of the law" (Rom. xiii. 8–10). "This commandment we have from Him, That he who loves God, love his brother also" (1 John iv. 21). "If ye fulfil the royal law, Thou shalt love thy neighbour as thyself, ye do well. But if ye have respect to persons ye commit sin, and are convinced of the law as transgressors" (James ii. 8, 9). "Circumcision is nothing, uncircumcision is nothing," comparatively speaking; "but," under Christ, "the keeping of the commandments of God" is the one thing needful (1 Cor. vii. 19). "For the end of the commandment is charity out of a pure heart, and of a good conscience, and of faith unfeigned" (1 Tim. i. 5). "Though I have all faith," etc., "and have not charity, I am nothing" (1 Cor. xiii. 2). "Whosoever shall keep the whole law" of liberty, "and yet offend in one point" (in uncharitable respect of persons), "he is guilty of all," etc. "So speak ye, and so do, as they that shall be judged by the law of liberty," which requires perfect love, and therefore makes no allowance for the least degree of uncharitableness (James ii. 10, 12).

When the right foot of your faith stands on these evangelical precepts and proclamations, lest she should stagger for want of a promise every way adequate to such weighty commandments, let her place her left foot upon the following promises, which are extracted from the Old Testament:—"The Lord thy God will circumcise thine heart, and the heart of thy seed, to love the Lord thy God with all thine heart, and with all thy soul, that thou mayest live" (Deut. xxx. 6). "Come now, and let us reason together, says the Lord: though your sins be as scarlet, they shall be as white as snow; though they be red like crimson, they shall be as wool" (Isaiah i. 18). That this promise chiefly refers to sanctification is evident—(1) From the verses which immediately precede it: "Make you clean," etc. "Cease to do evil, learn to do well," etc. And (2) From the verses which immediately follow it: "If ye be willing and obedient, ye shall eat the good of the land; but if ye refuse and rebel," or disobey, "ye shall be devoured with the sword." Again: "I will give them an heart to know Me, that I am the Lord: and they shall be My people, and I will be their God," in a new and peculiar manner: "for they shall return unto Me with their whole heart." "This shall be the covenant that I will make with the house of Israel: After those days, says the Lord, I will put My law in their inward parts, and write it in their hearts; and will be their God, and they shall be My people" (Jeremiah xxiv. 7; xxxi. 33). "Then will I sprinkle clean water upon you, and ye shall be clean: from all your filthiness, and from all your idols, will I cleanse you. A new heart also will I give you, and a new spirit will I put within you: and I will put away the heart of stone out of your flesh, and I will give you an heart of flesh. And I will put my Spirit within you, and cause you to walk in My statutes, and ye shall keep My judgments, and do them" (Ezekiel xxxii. 25-27).

And let nobody suppose that the promises of the "circumcision," the "cleansing," the "clean water," and the "Spirit" which are mentioned in these scriptures, and by which the hearts of believers are to be made "new," and God's law is to be so written therein, that they shall "keep His judgments and do them"; let none, I say, suppose that these glorious promises belong only to the Jews; for their full accomplishment peculiarly refers to the Christian dispensation. Besides, if sprinkling of the Spirit were sufficient, under the Jewish dispensation, to raise the plant of Jewish perfection in Jewish believers, how much more will the revelation of "the horn of our salvation," and the outpourings of the Spirit, raise the plant of Christian perfection in faithful Christian believers! And that this revelation of Christ in the Spirit, as well as in the flesh, these effusions of the water of life, these baptisms of fire, which burn up the chaff of sin, throughly purge God's spiritual floor, save us from all our uncleannesses, and deliver us from all our enemies; that these blessings, I say, are peculiarly promised to Christians, is demonstrable by the following cloud of New Testament declarations and promises:—

"Blessed be the Lord God of Israel; for He hath raised up an horn of salvation for us, as He spake by the mouth of His holy prophets, that we, being delivered out of the hands of our enemies, might serve Him without" unbelieving "fear," that is, with perfect love, "in holiness and righteousness before Him, all the days of our life" (Luke i. 68–75). "Blessed are the poor in Spirit," who "thirst after righteousness: for they shall be filled" (Matt. v. 3, 6). "If thou knewest the gift of God," etc., "thou wouldest have asked of Him, and He would have given thee living water."

"And the water that I shall give him, shall be in him a well of water springing up to everlasting life" (John iv. 10, 14). "Jesus stood and cried, saying, If any man thirst, let him come to Me and drink. He that believeth on Me," when I shall have ascended up on high, to receive gifts for men, "out of his belly shall flow rivers of living water," to cleanse his soul, and to keep it clean. "But this He spake of the Spirit, which they that believe on Him shall receive; for the Holy Ghost was not yet given" in such a manner as to raise the plant of Christian perfection, "because Jesus was not yet glorified," and His spiritual dispensation was not yet fully opened (John vii. 37, etc.).

Mr. Wesley, in his *Plain Account of Christian Perfection*, has published some excellent queries, and proposes them to those who deny perfection to be attainable in this life. They are close to the point, and therefore the two first attack the imperfectionists from the very ground on which I want you to stand. They run thus—"(1) Has there not been a larger measure of the Holy Spirit given under the gospel than under the Jewish dispensation? If not, in what sense was 'the Spirit not given' before Christ was 'glorified'? (John vii. 39). (2) Was that 'glory which followed the sufferings of Christ' (1 Peter i. 11) an external glory, or an internal, viz., the glory of holiness"? Always rest the doctrine of Christian perfection on the scriptural foundation, and it will stand as firm as revelation itself.

It is allowed on all sides, that the dispensation of John the Baptist exceeded that of the other prophets, because it immediately introduced the gospel of Christ, and because John was not only appointed to "preach the baptism of repentance," but also clearly to point out the very person of Christ, and to "give knowledge of salvation to God's people by the remission of sins" (Luke i. 77). And, nevertheless, John only promised the blessing of the Spirit, which Christ bestowed when He had received gifts for men. "I indeed," said John, "baptize you with water unto repentance: but He that cometh after me is mightier than I; He shall baptize you with the Holy Ghost, and with fire" (Matt. iii. 11). Such is the importance of this promise, that it is particularly recorded not only by the three other evangelists (see Mark i. 8, Luke iii. 16, and John i. 26), but also by our Lord Himself, who said, just before His ascension, "John truly baptized with water; but ye shall be baptized with the Holy Ghost not many days hence" (Acts i. 5).

So capital is this promise of the Spirit's stronger influences to raise the rare plant of Christian perfection, that when our Lord speaks of this promise He emphatically calls it "the promise of the Father"; because it shines among the other promises of the gospel of Christ, as the moon does among the stars. Thus, Acts i. 4: "Wait," says He, "for the promise of the Father, which ye have heard of Me." And again, Luke xxiv. 49: "Behold, I send the promise of My Father upon you." Agreeably to this, St. Peter says, "Jesus being by the right hand of God exalted, and having received of the Father the promise of the Holy Ghost, He has shed forth this." He has begun abundantly to fulfil "that which was spoken by the prophet Joel: And it shall come to pass in the last days, saith God, that I will pour out" (bestow a more abundant measure) "of my Spirit upon all flesh." "Therefore repent and be baptized," that is, make an open profession of your faith, "in the Name of the Lord Jesus for the remission of sins; and ye shall receive the gift of the Holy Ghost. For the promise is unto you, and to your children, and to as many as the Lord our God shall call" to enjoy the full blessings of the Christian dispensation (Acts ii. 16, 17, 33-39). This promise, when it is received in its fulness, is undoubtedly the greatest of all the "exceedingly great and precious promises" which "are given to us, that by them you might be partakers of the Divine nature," that is, of pure love and unmixed holiness (2 Peter i. 4). Have, therefore, a peculiar eye to it, and to these deep words of our Lord: "I will ask the Father, and He shall give you another Comforter, that He may abide with you for ever; even the Spirit of truth" and power, "whom the world knows not," etc.: "but ye know Him; for He remaineth with you, and shall be in you." "At that day ye shall know that I am in My Father, and you in Me, and I in you." For "if any man," that is, any believer, "love Me, he will keep My words: and My Father will love him, and we will come to him, and make our abode with him" (John xiv. 16-23). "Which," says Mr. Wesley, in his note on the place, "implies such a large manifestation of the Divine presence and love, that the former, in justification, is as nothing in comparison of it." Agreeably to this, the same judicious divine expresses himself thus in another of his publications:—"These virtues"—meekness, humility, and true resignation to God—"are the only wedding garment; they are the lamps and vessels well furnished with oil. There is nothing that will do instead of them; they must have their full and perfect work in you, or the soul can never be delivered from its fallen, wrathful state. There is no possibility of salvation but in this. And when the Lamb of God has brought forth His own meekness, etc., in our souls, then are our lamps trimmed, and our virgin hearts made ready for the marriage-feast. This marriage-feast signifies the entrance into the highest state of union that can be between God and the soul in this life. This birth-day of the Spirit of love in our souls, whenever we attain, will feast our souls with such peace and joy in God as will blot out the remembrance of every thing that we called peace or joy before."

To make you believe this important promise with more ardour, consider that our Lord spent some of His last moments in sealing it with His powerful intercession. After having prayed the Father to "sanctify" His disciples "through the truth" firmly embraced by their faith, and powerfully applied by His Spirit, He adds: "Neither pray I for these alone, but for them who will believe on Me through their word." And what is it that our Lord asks for these believers? Truly what St. Paul asked for the imperfect believers at Corinth, "even their perfection" (2 Cor. xiii. 9); a state of soul this, which Christ describes thus:— "That they all may be one; as Thou, Father, art in Me, and I in Thee, that they may be made one in us," etc.; "that they may be one, as we are one: I in them, and Thou in me, that they may be perfected in one; and that the world may know that Thou hast loved them as Thou hast loved me" (John xvii. 17–23). Our Lord could not pray in vain: it is not to be supposed that the Scriptures are silent with respect to the effect of this solemn prayer, an answer to which was to give the world an idea of the New Jerusalem coming down from heaven,—a specimen of the power which introduces believers into the state of Christian perfection; and therefore we read that, on the day of Pentecost, the kingdom of Satan was powerfully shaken, and the kingdom of God—"righteousness, peace, and joy in the Holy Ghost"— began to come with a new power. Then were thousands wonderfully converted, and clearly justified. Then was the kingdom of heaven taken by force; and the love of

Christ, and of the brethren, began to burn the chaff of selfishness and sin with a force which the world had never seen before. (See Acts ii. 42, etc.) Some time after, another glorious baptism, or capital outpouring of the Spirit, carried believers farther into the kingdom of the grace which perfects them in one. And therefore we find that the account which St. Luke gives us of them after this second capital manifestation of the Holy Spirit, in a great degree answers to our Lord's prayer for their perfection. He had asked "that they all might be one," that they "might be one as the Father and He are one," and that they "might be perfected in one" (John xvii. 17, etc.). And now a fuller answer is given to His deep request. Take it in the words of the inspired historian:—"And when they had prayed, the place was shaken where they were assembled together; and they were" once more "filled with the Holy Ghost, and they spake the word with" still greater "boldness. And the multitude of them that believed were of one heart, and of one soul: neither said any of them, that aught of the things which he possessed was his own; but they had all things common,".etc. "And great grace was upon them all" (Acts iv. 31–33). Who does not see in this account a specimen of that grace which our Lord had asked for believers, when He had prayed that His disciples, and those who would believe on Him through their word, might be "perfected in one"!

It may be asked here, whether the multitude of them that believed in those happy days were all perfect in love. I answer, that if pure love had cast out all selfishness and sinful fear from their hearts, they were undoubtedly made perfect in love. But as God does not usually remove the plague of indwelling sin till it has been discovered and lamented; and as we find, in the two next chapters, an account of the guile of Ananias and his wife, and of the partiality or selfish murmuring of some believers, it seems that those chiefly who before were strong in the grace of their dispensation arose then into sinless fathers; and that the first love of other believers, through the peculiar blessing of Christ upon His infant Church, was so bright and powerful for a time, that little children had, or seemed to have, the strength of young men, and young men the grace of fathers. And, in this case, the account which St. Luke gives of the primitive believers ought to be taken with some restriction: thus, while many of them were perfect in love, many might have the imperfection of their love only covered over by a land-flood of "peace and joy in believing." And, in this case, what is said of their being "all of one heart and mind," and of their "having all things common," etc., may only mean that the harmony of love had not yet been broken, and that none had yet betrayed any of the uncharitableness for which Christians in after ages became so conspicuous. With respect to the "great grace" which "was upon them all," this does not necessarily mean that they were all equally strong in grace; for great unity and happiness may rest upon a whole family, where the difference between a father, a young man, and a child continues to subsist. However, it is not improbable that God, to open the dispensation of the Spirit in a manner which might fix the attention of all ages upon its importance and glory, permitted the whole body of believers to take an extraordinary turn together into the Canaan of perfect love, and to show the world the admirable fruit which grows there, as the spies sent by Joshua took a turn into the good land of promise before they were settled in it, and brought from thence the bunch of grapes which astonished and spirited up the Israelites who had not yet crossed Jordan.

Upon the whole, it is, I think, undeniable, from the four first chapters of the Acts, that a peculiar power of the Spirit is bestowed upon believers, under the gospel of Christ; that this power, through faith on our part, can operate the most sudden and surprising change in our souls; and that, when our faith shall fully embrace the promise of full sanctification, or of a complete circumcision of the heart in the Spirit, the Holy Ghost, who kindled so much love on the day of Pentecost, that all the primitive believers loved, or seemed to love, each other perfectly, will not fail to help us to "love one another" without sinful self-seeking;

and as soon as we do so "God dwelleth in us, and His love is perfected in us" (1 John iv. 12; John xiv. 23).

Should you ask, "How many baptisms, or effusions of the sanctifying Spirit, are necessary to cleanse a believer from all sin, and to kindle his soul into perfect love?" I reply, that the effect of a sanctifying truth depending upon the ardour of the faith with which that truth is embraced, and upon the power of the Spirit with which it is applied, I should betray a want of modesty if I brought the operations of the Holy Ghost, and the energy of faith, under a rule which is not expressly laid down in Scripture. If you asked your physician how many doses of physic you must take before all the crudities of your stomach can be carried off, and your appetite perfectly restored, he would probably answer you, that this depends upon the nature of those crudities, the strength of the medicine, and the manner in which your constitution will allow it to operate; and that, in general, you must repeat the dose, as you can bear, till the remedy has fully answered the desired end. I return a similar answer: If one powerful baptism of the Spirit "seals you unto the day of redemption," and "cleanses you from all" moral "filthiness," so much the better. If two or more are necessary, the Lord can repeat them; "His arm is not shortened that it cannot save," nor is His promise of the Spirit stinted: He says, in general, "Whosoever will, let him come and take of the water of life freely." "If you, being evil, know how to give good gifts to your children, how much more will your heavenly Father," who is goodness itself, "give His holy" sanctifying "Spirit to them that ask Him"? I may, however, venture to say, in general, that, before we can rank among perfect Christians, we must receive so much of the truth and Spirit of Christ by faith, as to have the pure love of God and man shed abroad in our hearts by the Holy Ghost given unto us, and to be filled with the meek and lowly mind which was in Christ. And if one outpouring of the Spirit, one bright manifestation of the sanctifying truth, so empties us of self as to fill us with the mind of Christ, and with pure love, we are undoubtedly Christians, in the full sense of the word. From the ground of my soul, I therefore subscribe to the answer which a great divine makes to the following objection:—

"But some who are newly justified do come up to this" (Christian perfection). "What, then, will you say to these?" Mr. Wesley replies with great propriety: "If they really do, I will say, They are sanctified, saved from sin in that moment; and that they never need lose what God has given, or feel sin any more. But certainly this is an exempt case: it is otherwise with the generality of those that are justified; they feel in themselves more or less pride, anger, self-will, and a heart bent to backsliding; and till they have gradually mortified these, they are not fully renewed in love. God usually gives a considerable time for men to receive light, to grow in grace, to do and suffer His will, before they are either justified or sanctified. But He does not invariably adhere to this; sometimes He cuts short His work; He does the work of many years in a few weeks, perhaps in a week, a day, an hour. He justifies or sanctifies both those who have done or suffered nothing, and who have not had time for a gradual growth either in light or grace. And may He not do what He will with His own? 'Is thine eye evil, because He is good?' It need not, therefore, be proved by forty texts of Scripture, either that most men are perfected in love at last, or that there is a gradual work of God in the soul; and that, generally speaking, it is a long time, even many years, before sin is destroyed. All this we know; but we know, likewise, that God may, with man's good leave, cut short His work, in whatever degree He pleases, and do the usual work of many years in a moment. He does so in many instances: and yet there is a gradual work both before and after that moment; so that one may affirm the work is gradual, another it is instantaneous, without any manner of contradiction." The same eminent divine explains himself more fully thus: "It" (Christian perfection) "is constantly preceded and followed by a gradual work. But is it in itself instantaneous or not? In examining this, let us go on step by step. An instantaneous change has been wrought in some believers: none can deny this. Since that change they enjoy perfect love; they feel this, and this alone; they rejoice evermore, pray without ceasing, in everything give thanks. Now, this is all that I mean by 'perfection'; therefore these are witnesses of the perfection which I preach. 'But in some this change was not instantaneous.' They did not perceive the instant when it was wrought; it is often difficult to perceive the instant when a man dies! yet there is an instant in which life ceases: and if ever sin ceases, there must be a last moment of its existence, and a first moment of our deliverance from it. 'But if they have this love now, they will lose it.' They may; but they need not. And whether they do or no, they have it now; they now experience what we teach; they now are all love; they now rejoice, pray, and praise without ceasing. 'However, sin is only suspended in them, it is not destroyed.' Call it which you please, they are all love to-day, and they 'take no thought for the morrow.'" To return:

2. When you firmly assent to the truth of the precepts and promises on which the doctrine of Christian perfection is founded; when you understand the meaning of these scriptures—"Sanctify them through Thy truth: Thy word is truth"; "I will send the Comforter" (the Spirit of truth and holiness) "unto you"; "God has chosen you to" eternal "salvation, through sanctification of the

Spirit, and belief of the truth,"—when you see that the way to Christian perfection is by the word of the gospel of Christ, by faith, and by the Spirit of God: in the next place, get tolerably clear ideas of this perfection. This is absolutely necessary. If you will hit a mark, you must know where it is. Some people aim at Christian perfection, but, mistaking it for angelical perfection, they shoot above the mark, miss it, and then peevishly give up their hopes. Others place the mark as much too low: hence it is that you hear them profess to have attained Christian perfection, when they have not so much as attained the mental serenity of a philosopher, or the candour of a good-natured, conscientious heathen. In the preceding pages, if I am not mistaken, the mark is fixed according to the rules of scriptural moderation: it is not placed so high as to make you despair of hitting it, if you do your best in an evangelical manner; nor yet so low as to allow you to presume that you can reach it without exerting all your abilities to the uttermost, in due subordination to the efficacy of Jesus's blood, and the Spirit's sanctifying influences.

3. Should ye ask, "Which is the way to Christian perfection? Shall we go to it by internal stillness, agreeably to this direction of Moses and David?—'The Lord will fight for you, and ye shall hold your peace. Stand still, and see the salvation of God.' 'Be still, and know that I am God.' 'Stand in awe, and

sin not: commune with your own heart upon your bed, and be still.' Or shall we press after it by an internal wrestling, according to these commands of Christ?— 'Strive to enter in at the strait gate.' 'The kingdom of heaven suffereth violence, and the violent taketh it by force,'" etc.

According to the evangelical balance of the doctrine of free grace and free will, I answer, that the way to perfection is by the due combination of prevenient, assisting free grace, and of submissive, assisted free will. Antinomian stillness, therefore, which says that free grace must do all, is not the way; pharisaic activity, which will do most, if not all, is not the way. Join these two partial systems, allowing free grace the lead and high pre-eminence which it so justly claims, and you have the balance of the two gospel axioms; you do justice to the doctrines of mercy and justice, of free grace and free will, of divine faithfulness, in keeping the covenant of grace, and of human faithfulness, in laying hold on that covenant, and keeping within its bounds: in short, you have the Scripture method of waiting upon God, which Mr. Wesley describes thus—

"Restless, resign'd, for God I wait;
For God my vehement soul stands still."

To understand these lines, consider that faith, like the Virgin Mary, is alternately a receiver and a bestower: first, it passively receives the impregnation of divine grace, saying, "Behold the handmaid of the Lord: let it be done to me according to

Thy word"; and then it actively brings forth its heavenly fruit with earnest labour. "God worketh in you to will and to do," says St. Paul. Here he describes the passive office of faith, which submits to, and acquiesces in, every divine dispensation and operation. "Therefore work out your own salvation with fear and trembling," and, of consequence, with haste, diligence, ardour, and faithfulness. Here the apostle describes the active office of that mother-grace, which carefully lays out the talent she has already received. Would ye then wait aright for Christian perfection? Impartially admit the two gospel axioms, and faithfully reduce them to practice. In order to this, let them meet in your hearts, as the two legs of a pair of compasses meet in the rivet which makes them one compound instrument. Let your faith in the doctrine of free grace, and Christ's righteousness, fix your mind upon God as you fix one of the legs of your compasses immovably in the centre of the circle which you are about to draw; so shall you stand still according to the first texts produced in the question. And then, let your faith in the doctrine of free will and evangelical obedience make you steadily run the circle of duty around that firm centre; so shall you imitate the other leg of the compasses, which evenly moves around the centre, and traces the circumference of a perfect circle. By this activity subordinate to grace, you will "take the kingdom of heaven by force." When your heart quietly rests in God by faith, as it steadily acts the part of a passive receiver, it resembles the leg of the compasses which rests in the centre of the circle; and then the poet's expressions, "restless, resigned," describe its fixedness in God. But when your heart swiftly moves towards God by faith, as it acts the part of a diligent worker; when your ardent soul follows after God, as a thirsty deer does after the water-brooks, it may be compared to the leg of the compasses which traces the circumference of the circle: and then these words of the poet, "restless" and "vehement," properly belong to it. To go on steadily to perfection, you must therefore endeavour steadily to believe, according to the doctrine of the first gospel axiom; and, as there is opportunity, diligently to work, according to the doctrine of the second. And the moment your faith is steadily fixed in God as in your centre, and your obedience swiftly moves in the circle of duty from the rest and power which you find in that centre you have attained, you are made perfect in the faith which works by love. Your humble faith saves you from pharisaism, your obedient love from antinomianism; and both, in due subordination to Christ, constitute you a just man made perfect according to dispensation.

4. Another question has also puzzled many sincere perfectionists; and the solution of it may remove a considerable hindrance out of your way. "Is Christian perfection," say they, "to be instantaneously brought down to us? or are we gradually

to grow up to it? Shall we be made perfect in love by a habit of holiness suddenly infused into us, or by acts of feeble faith and feeble love so frequently repeated as to become strong, habitual, and evangelically natural to us, according to the well-known maxim, 'A strong habit is a second nature'?"

Both ways are good; and instances of some believers gradually perfected, and of others, comparatively speaking, instantaneously fixed in perfect love, might probably be produced, if we were acquainted with the experiences of all those who have died in a state of evangelical perfection. It may be with the root of sin, as it is with its fruit: some souls parley many years, before they can be persuaded to give up all their outward sins; and others part with them as it were instantaneously. You may compare the former to those besieged towns which make a long resistance, or to those mothers who go through a tedious and lingering labour; and the latter resemble those fortresses which are surprised and carried by storm, or those women who are delivered almost as soon as labour comes upon them. Travellers inform us that vegetation is so quick and powerful in some warm climates, that the seeds of some vegetables yield a salad in less than twenty-four hours. Should a northern philosopher say "Impossible!" and should an English gardener exclaim against such mushroom salad, they would only expose their prejudices, as do those who decry instantaneous justification, or mock at the possibility of the instantaneous destruction of indwelling sin.

For where is the absurdity of this doctrine? If the light of a candle brought into a dark room can instantly expel the darkness; and if, upon opening your shutters at noon, your gloomy apartment can instantaneously be filled with meridian light, why might not the instantaneous rending of the veil of unbelief, or the sudden and full opening of the eye of your faith, instantly fill your soul with the light of truth, and the fire of love; supposing the Sun of Righteousness arise upon you with powerful healing in His wings? May not the Sanctifier descend upon your waiting soul as quickly as the Spirit descended upon our Lord at His baptism? Did it not descend as a dove, that is, with the soft motion of a dove, which swiftly shoots down, and instantly lights? A good man said once, with truth, "A mote is little when it is compared to the sun; but I am far less before God." Alluding to this comparison, I ask, If the sun could instantly kindle a mote; nay, if a burning glass can in a moment calcine a bone, and turn a stone to lime; and if the dim flame of a candle can in the twinkling of an eye destroy the flying insect which comes within its sphere, how unscriptural and irrational is it to suppose, that when God fully baptizes a soul with His sanctifying Spirit and with the celestial fire of His love, He cannot in an instant destroy the man of sin, burn up the chaff of corruption, melt the heart of stone into a heart of flesh, and kindle the believing soul into pure seraphic love!

An appeal to parallel cases may throw some light upon the question which I answer. If you were sick, and asked of God the perfect recovery of your health, how would you look for it? Would you expect to have your strength restored you at once, without any external means, as the lepers who were instantly cleansed; and as the paralytic, who, at our Lord's word, took up the bed on which he lay, and carried it away upon his shoulders; or, by using some external means of a slower operation, as the "ten lepers" did, who were more gradually cleansed "as they went to show themselves to the priests"? or, as King Hezekiah, whose gradual but equally sure recovery was owing to God's blessing upon the poultice of figs prescribed by Isaiah? Again: if you were blind, and besought the Lord to give you perfect human sight, how should you wait for it? as Bartimeus, whose eyes were opened in an instant? or, as the man who received his sight by degrees? At first he saw nothing; by and by he confusedly discovered the objects before him; but at last he "saw all things clearly"! Would ye not earnestly wait for an answer to your prayers now; leaving to Divine wisdom the particular manner of your recovery? And why should ye not go and do likewise, with respect to the dreadful disorder which we call indwelling sin?

If our hearts are "purified by faith," as

the Scripture expressly testifies; if the faith which peculiarly purifies the heart of Christians is a faith in "the promise of the Father," which promise was made by the Son, and directly points at a peculiar effusion of the Holy Ghost, the purifier of spirits; if we may believe in a moment; and if God may, in a moment, seal our sanctifying faith by sending us a fulness of His sanctifying Spirit;—if this, I say, is the case, does it not follow, that to deny the possibility of the instantaneous destruction of sin is to deny, contrary to Scripture and matter of fact, that we can make an instantaneous act of faith in the sanctifying promise of the Father, and in the all-cleansing blood of the Son, and that God can seal that act by the instantaneous operation of His Spirit? which St. Paul calls "the circumcision of the heart in" or by "the Spirit," according to the Lord's ancient promise: "I will circumcise thy heart, to love the Lord thy God with all thy heart." Where is the absurdity of believing that the God of all grace can now give an answer to the poet's rational and evangelical request?—

"Open my faith's interior eye;
Display Thy glory from above,
And sinful self shall sink and die,
Lost in astonishment and love."

If a momentary display of Christ's bodily glory could in an instant turn Saul, the blaspheming, bloody persecutor, into Paul, the praying, gentle apostle; if a sudden sight of Christ's hands could, in a moment, root up from Thomas's heart that detestable resolution, "I will not believe," and produce that deep confession of faith, "My Lord and my God!" what cannot the display of Christ's spiritual glory operate in a believing soul, to which He manifests Himself, "according to that power whereby He is able to subdue all things to Himself"? Again: if Christ's body could, in an instant, become so glorious on the mount, that His very garments partook of the sudden irradiation, became not only free from every spot, but also "white as the light," "shining exceeding white as snow, so as no fuller on earth can white them"; and if our bodies "shall be changed," if "this corruptible shall put on incorruption, and this mortal shall put on immortality, in a moment, in the twinkling of an eye, at the last trump," why may not our believing souls, when they fully submit to God's terms, be fully changed, fully "turned from the power" of Satan unto God? When the Holy Ghost says, "Now is the day of salvation," does He exclude salvation from heart iniquity? If Christ now deserves fully the name of "Jesus, because He" fully "saves His" believing "people from their sins"; and if now the gospel trumpet sounds, and sinners arise from the dead, why should we not, upon the performance of the conditions, be changed in a moment from indwelling sin to indwelling holiness? Why should we not pass in the twinkling of an eye, or in a short time, from indwelling death to indwelling life?

This is not all: if you deny the possibility of a quick destruction of indwelling sin, you send to hell, or to some unscriptural purgatory, not only the dying thief, but also all those martyrs who suddenly embraced the Christian faith, and were instantly put to death by bloody persecutors for confessing the faith which they had just embraced. And if you allow that God may "cut His work short in righteousness" in such a case, why not in other cases? why not, especially, when a believer confesses his indwelling sin, ardently prays that Christ would, and sincerely believes that Christ can, now "cleanse from all unrighteousness"?

Nobody is so apt to laugh at the instantaneous destruction of sin as the Calvinists; and yet, such is the inconsistency which characterises some men, their doctrine of purgatory is built upon it. For, if you credit them, all dying believers have a nature which is still morally corrupted, and a heart which is yet desperately wicked. These believers, still full of indwelling sin, instantaneously breathe out their last, and, without any peculiar act of faith, without any peculiar outpouring of the sanctifying Spirit, corruption is instantaneously gone. The indwelling man of sin has passed through the Geneva purgatory, he is entirely consumed; and, behold! the souls which would not hear of the instantaneous act of sanctifying faith which receives the indwelling Spirit of holiness,—the souls which pleaded hard for the continuance of indwelling sin,—are now completely sinless; and in the twinkling of an eye they appear in the third heaven among the spirits of just Christians made perfect in love! Such is the doctrine of our opponents; and yet they think it incredible that God should do for us, while we pray in faith, what they suppose death will do for them, when they lie in his cold arms, perhaps delirious or senseless.

On the other hand, to deny that imperfect believers may and do gradually grow in grace, and, of course, that the remains of their sins may and do gradually decay, is as absurd as to deny that God waters the earth by daily dews, as well as by thunder showers: it is as ridiculous as to assert that nobody is carried off by lingering disorders, but that all men die suddenly, or a few hours after they are taken ill.

I use these comparisons about death, to throw some light upon the question which I solve, and not to insinuate that the decay and destruction of sin run parallel to the decay and dissolution of the body, and that, of course, sin must end with our bodily life. Were I to admit this unscriptural tenet, I should build again what I have all along endeavoured to destroy; and, as I love consistency, I should promise eternal salvation to all unbelievers,—for unbelievers, I presume, will die, that is, will go into the Geneva purgatory, as well as believers. Nor do I see why death should not be able to destroy the van and the main body of sin's forces, if it can so readily cut the rear—the remains of sin—in pieces.

From the preceding observations it appears that believers generally go to Christian perfection, as the disciples went to the other side of the Sea of Galilee,—they toiled some time very hard, and with little success; but, after they had "rowed about twenty-five or thirty furlongs, they saw Jesus walking on the sea. He said to them, It is I; be not afraid. Then they willingly received Him into the ship; and immediately the ship was at the land whither they went." Just so we toil till our faith discovers Christ in the promise, and welcomes Him into our hearts; and such is the effect of His presence, that immediately we arrive at the land of perfection. Or, to use another illustration, God says to believers, "Go to the Canaan of perfect love. Arise; why do ye tarry? Wash away the remains of sin, calling," that is, believing, "on the Name of the Lord." And if they submit to the obedience of faith, He deals with them as He did with the evangelist Philip, to whom He had said, "Arise, and go towards the south"; for, when they arise and run, as Philip did, the Spirit of the Lord takes them, as He did the evangelist, and they are found in the New Jerusalem, as "Philip was found at Azotus." They dwell in God, or in perfect love; and God, or perfect love, dwells in them.

Hence it follows, that the most evangelical method of following after the perfection to which we are immediately called is, that of seeking it now, by endeavouring fully to lay hold on the promise of that perfection, through faith, just as if our repeated acts of obedience could never help us forward. But, in the meantime, we should do the work of faith, and repeat our internal and external acts of obedience, with as much earnestness and faithfulness, according to our present power, as if we were sure to enter into rest merely by a diligent use of our talents and a faithful exertion of the powers which divine grace has bestowed upon us. If we do not attend to the first of these directions, we shall seek to be sanctified by works, like the pharisees; and if we disregard the second, we shall slide into solifidian sloth with the antinomians.

This double direction is founded upon the connection of the two gospel axioms. If the second axiom, which implies the doctrine of free will, were false, I would only say, Be still; or rather, do nothing: free grace alone will do all in you and for you. But as this axiom is as true as the first, I must add, Strive in humble subordination to free grace; for Christ saith, "To him that hath" initiating grace to purpose, more grace "shall be given, and he shall have abundance"; his faithful and equitable Benefactor will give him the reward of perfecting grace.

5. Beware, therefore, of unscriptural refinements. Set out for the Canaan of perfect love, with a firm resolution to labour for the rest which remains on earth for the people of God. Some good,

mistaken men, "wise above what is written," and fond of striking out paths which were unknown to the apostles,— new paths, marked out by voluntary humility, and leading to antinomianism,— some people of that stamp, I say, have made it their business, from the days of heated Augustine, to decry making resolutions. They represent this practice as a branch of what they are pleased to call "legality." They insinuate that it is utterly inconsistent with the knowledge of our inconstancy and weakness. In a word, they frighten us from the first step to Christian perfection,—from a humble, evangelical determination to run till we reach the prize, or, if you please, to go down till we come to the lowest place. It may not be amiss to point out the ground of their mistake. Once they broke the balance of the gospel axioms, by leaning too much towards free will, and by not laying their first and principal stress upon free grace. God, to bring them to the evangelical mean, refused His blessing to their unevangelical willing and running: hence it is that their self-righteous resolutions "started aside like a broken bow." When they found out their mistake, instead of coming back to the line of moderation, they fled to the other extreme: casting all their weights into the scale of free grace, they absurdly formed a resolution never to form a resolution; and, determining not to throw one determination into the scale of free will, they began to draw all the believers they met with into the ditch of a slothful quietism and Laodicean stillness.

You will never steadily go on to perfection, unless you get over this mistake. Let the imperfectionists laugh at you for making humble resolutions; but go on, "steadfastly purposing to lead a new life," as says our Church: and in order to this, steadfastly purpose to get a new heart, in the full sense of the word; for, so long as your heart will continue partly unrenewed, your life will be partly unholy; and therefore St. James justly observes, that "if any man offend not in word, he is a perfect man," he loves God with all his heart, his heart is fully renewed, it being impossible that a heart still tainted in part with vanity and guile should always dictate the words of sincerity and love. Your good resolutions need not fail; nor will they fail, if, under a due sense of the fickleness and helplessness of your unassisted free will, you properly depend upon God's faithfulness and assistance. However, should they fail, as they probably will do, more than once, be not discouraged, but repent, search out the cause, and, in the strength of free grace, let your assisted free will renew your evangelical purpose, till the Lord seals it with His mighty fiat, and says, "Let it be done to thee according to thy" resolving "faith." It is much better to be laughed at as "poor creatures who know nothing of themselves," than to be deluded as foolish virgins, who fondly imagine that their vessels are full of imputed oil. Take, therefore, "the sword of the Spirit," and boldly cut this dangerous snare in pieces. Conscious of your impotence, and yet laying out your talent of free will, say with the prodigal son, "I will arise, and go to my Father." Say with David, "I will love Thee, O Lord my God." "I will behold Thy face in righteousness." "I am purposed that my mouth shall not transgress; I will keep it as it were with a bridle." "I have said that I would keep Thy word." "The proud," and they who are humble in an unscriptural way, "have had me exceedingly in derision; but I will keep Thy precepts with my whole heart." "I have sworn, and I will perform it, that I will keep Thy righteous judgments." Say with St. Paul, "I am determined not to know anything, save Jesus, and Him crucified"; and with Jacob, "I will not let Thee go, unless Thou bless me." And, to sum up all good resolutions in one, if you are a member of the Church of England, say, "I have engaged to renounce all the vanities of this wicked world, all the sinful lusts of the flesh, and all the works of the devil; to believe all the articles of the Christian faith; and to keep God's commandments all the days of my life; that is, I have most solemnly resolved to be a perfect Christian; and this resolution I have publicly sealed, by receiving the two sacraments upon it, — Baptism, after my parents and sponsors had laid me under this blessed vow,—and the Lord's Supper, after I had personally ratified, in the bishop's presence, what they had done.

Nor do I only think that I am bound to keep this vow, but 'by God's grace, so I will; and I heartily thank our heavenly Father, that He has called me to this state of salvation' and Christian perfection; 'and I pray unto Him, to give me His grace, that I may' not only attain it, but also 'continue in the same unto my life's end.'"—*Church Catechism.*

"Much diligence," says Kempis, "is necessary to him that will profit much. If he who firmly purposeth often faileth, what shall he do who seldom or feebly purposeth anything?" But, I say it again and again, do not lean upon your free will and good purposes, so as to encroach upon the glorious pre-eminence of free grace. Let the first gospel axiom stand invariably in its honourable place. Lay your principal stress upon divine mercy; and say, with the good man whom I have just quoted, "Help me, O Lord God, in Thy holy service, and grant that I may now this day begin perfectly."

In following this method, ye will do the two gospel axioms justice: ye will so depend upon God's free grace, as not to fall into pharisaic running; and ye will so exert your own free will, as not to slide into antinomian sloth. Your course lies exactly between these rocks. To pass these perilous straits, your resolving heart must acquire a heavenly polarity. Through the spiritually magnetic touch of Christ, "the corner-stone," your soul must learn to point towards faith and works, or, if you please, towards a due submission to free grace, and a due exertion of free will, as the opposite ends of the needle of a compass point towards the north and the south.

6. From this direction flows the following advice:—Resolve to be perfect in yourselves, but not of yourselves. The antinomians boast that they are perfect only in their heavenly Representative. Christ was filled with perfect humility and love; they are perfect in His person; they need not a perfection of humble love in themselves. To avoid their error, be perfect in yourselves, and not in another; let your perfection of humility and love be inherent; let it dwell in you. Let it fill your own heart, and influence your own life; so shall you avoid the delusion of the virgins, who give you to understand that the oil of their perfection is all contained in that sacred vessel which formerly hung on the cross, and therefore their salvation is finished; they have oil enough in that rich vessel, manna enough and to spare in that golden pot. Christ's heart was perfect; and theirs may safely remain imperfect, yea, full of indwelling sin, till death, the messenger of the Bridegroom, come to cleanse them, and fill them with perfect love at the midnight cry. Delusive hope! Can anything be more absurd than for a sapless, dry branch to fancy that it has sap and moisture enough in the vine which it cumbers? or for an impenitent adulterer to boast that "in the Lord he has" chastity and "righteousness"? Where did Christ ever

say, "Have salt in another"? Does He not say, "Take heed that ye be not deceived"? "Have salt in yourselves"? (Mark ix. 50). Does He not impute the destruction of stony ground hearers to their "not having root in themselves"? (Matt. xiii. 21). If it was the patient man's comfort, that "the root of the matter was found in him," is it not deplorable to hear modern believers say, without any explanatory clause, that they have nothing but sin in themselves? But is it enough to have the root in ourselves? Must we not also have "the fruit"; yea, "be filled with the fruits of righteousness"? (Phil. i. 11). Is it not St. Peter's doctrine, where he says, "If these things be in you, and abound, ye shall neither be barren, nor unfruitful in the knowledge of Christ"? (2 Peter i. 8). And is it not that of David where he prays, "Create in me a clean heart"? etc. Away, then, with all antinomian refinements; and if, with St. Paul, you will have salvation and rejoicing in yourselves, and not in another, make sure of holiness and perfection in yourselves, and not in another.

But while you endeavour to avoid the snare of the antinomians, do not run into that of the pharisees, who will have their perfection of themselves, and therefore, by their own unevangelical efforts, self-concerted willings, and self-prescribed runnings, endeavour to "raise sparks of their own kindling," and to "warm themselves by" their own painted fires, and fruitless agitations. Feel your impotence. Own that "no man hath quickened" and perfected "his own soul." Be contented to invite, receive, and welcome the light of life; but never attempt to reform or to engross it. It is your duty to wait for the morning light, and to rejoice when it visits you: but if you grow so self-conceited as to say, "I will create a sun: let there be light"; or if, when the light visits your eyes, you say, "I will bear a stock of light; I will so fill my eyes with light to-day, that to-morrow I shall almost be able to do my work without the sun, or at least without a constant dependence upon its beams," would ye not betray a species of self-deifying idolatry and satanical pride? If our Lord Himself, as "Son of Man," would not have one grain of human goodness of Himself; if He said, "Why callest thou Me good? there is none good," self-good, or good of Himself, "but God," who can wonder enough at those proud Christians, who claim some self-originated goodness, boasting of what they have received, as if they had not received it; or using what they have received, without a humble sense of their constant dependence upon their heavenly Benefactor? To avoid this horrid delusion of the pharisees, learn to see, to feel, and to acknowledge that of the Father, through the Son, and by the Holy Ghost, are all your Urim and Thummim, your "lights" and "perfections." And while the Lord says, "From Me is thy fruit found" (Hosea xiv. 8), bow at His footstool, and gratefully reply,

"Of Thy fulness have all we received, and grace for grace" (John i. 16). For Thou art "the Father of lights, from whom cometh every good and perfect gift" (James i. 17). "Of Thee, and through Thee, and to Thee, are all things. To Thee," therefore, "be the glory for ever. Amen" (Rom. xi. 36).

7. You will have this humble and thankful disposition, if you let your repentance cast deeper roots. For if Christian perfection implies a forsaking all inward as well as outward sin; and if true repentance is a grace "whereby we forsake sin," it follows, that, to attain Christian perfection, we must so follow our Lord's evangelical precept, "Repent, for the kingdom of heaven is at hand," as to leave no sin, no bosom sin, no heart sin, no indwelling sin, unrepented of, and, of consequence, unforsaken. He whose heart is still full of indwelling sin has no more truly repented of indwelling sin, than the man whose mouth is still defiled with filthy talking and jesting has truly repented of his ribaldry. The deeper our sorrow for and detestation of indwelling sin is, the more penitently do we confess "the plague of our heart"; and when we properly confess it, we inherit the blessing promised in these words: "If we confess our sins, He is faithful and just to forgive us our sins, and to cleanse us from all unrighteousness."

To promote this deep repentance, consider how many spiritual evils still haunt your breast. Look into the inward chamber of imagery, where assuming self-love, surrounded by a multitude of vain thoughts, foolish desires, and wild imaginations, keeps her court. Grieve that your heart, which should be all flesh, is yet partly stone; that your soul, which should be only a temple for the Holy Ghost, is yet so frequently turned into a den of thieves, a hole for the cockatrice, a nest for a brood of spiritual vipers—for the remains of envy, jealousy, fretfulness, anger, pride, impatience, peevishness, formality, sloth, prejudice, bigotry, carnal confidence, evil shame, self-righteousness, tormenting fears, uncharitable suspicions, idolatrous love, and I know not how many of the evils which form the retinue of hypocrisy and unbelief. Through grace, detect these evils by a close attention to what passes in your own heart at all times, but especially in an hour of temptation. By frequent and deep confession, drag out all these abominations; these sins, which would not have Christ to reign alone over you, bring before Him, place them in the light of His countenance; and, if you do it in faith, that light, and the warmth of His love, will kill them, as the light and heat of the sun kill the worms which the plough turns up to the open air in a dry summer's day.

Nor plead that you can do nothing; for, by the help of Christ, who is always ready to assist the helpless, ye can solemnly say upon your knees, what ye have probably said in an airy manner to your professing friends. If ye ever acknowledged to them that your heart is deceitful, prone to leave undone what ye ought to do, and ready to do what ye ought to leave undone, ye can undoubtedly make the same confession to God. Complain to Him who can help you, as ye have done to those who cannot; lament, as you are able, the darkness of your mind, the stiffness of your will, the dulness or exorbitancy of your affections; and importunately entreat the God of all grace to renew a right spirit within you. If ye "sorrow after this godly sort, what carefulness" will be "wrought in you, what indignation, what fear, what vehement desire, what zeal, yea, what revenge"! Ye will then sing in faith what the imperfectionists sing in unbelief:—

"O how I hate those lusts of mine
    That crucified my God ;
Those sins that pierced and nail'd His flesh
    Fast to the fatal wood!

Yes, my Redeemer, they shall die,
    My heart hath so decreed ;
Nor will I spare those guilty things
    That made my Saviour bleed.

Whilst with a melting, broken heart,
    My murder'd Lord I view,
I'll raise revenge against my sins,
    And slay the murderers too."

8. Closely connected with this deep repentance is the practice of a judicious, universal self-denial. "If thou wilt be perfect," says our Lord, "deny thyself, take up thy cross daily and follow Me."

"He that loveth father or mother," much more, he that loveth praise, pleasure, or money, "more than Me, is not worthy of Me." Nay, "whosoever will save his life, shall lose it; and whosoever will lose it for My sake, shall find it." Many desire to live and reign with Christ, but few choose to suffer and die with Him. However, as the way of the cross leads to heaven, it undoubtedly leads to Christian perfection. To avoid the cross, therefore, or to decline drinking the cup of vinegar and gall which God permits your friends or foes to mix for you, is to throw away the aloes which divine wisdom puts to the breasts of the mother of harlots, to wean you from her and her witchcrafts; it is to refuse a medicine which is kindly prepared to restore your health and appetite;—in a word, it is to renounce the Physician who heals all our infirmities, when we take His bitter draughts, submit to have our imposthumes opened by His sharp lancet, and yield to have our proud flesh wasted away by His painful caustics. Our Lord "was made" a "perfect" Saviour "through sufferings"; and we may be made perfect Christians in the same manner; we may be called to suffer, till all that which we have brought out of spiritual Egypt is consumed in a howling wilderness, in a dismal Gethsemane, or on a shameful Calvary. Should this lot be reserved for us, let us not imitate our Lord's imperfect disciples, who "forsook Him, and fled"; but let us stand the fiery trial, till all our fetters are melted, and all our dross is purged away. Fire is of a purgative nature; it separates the dross from the gold; and the fiercer it is, the more quick and powerful is its operation. "He that is left in Zion, and he that remaineth in Jerusalem, shall be called holy," etc., "when the Lord shall have washed away the filth of the daughters of Zion, and shall have purged the blood of Jerusalem, by the spirit of judgment and by the spirit of burning" (Isaiah iv. 3, 4). "I will bring the third part through the fire," saith the Lord, "and will refine them as silver is refined, and will try them as gold is tried: they shall call on My name, and I will hear them; I will say, It is My people; and they shall say, The Lord is my God" (Zech. xiii. 9). Therefore, if the Lord should suffer the best men in His camp, or the strongest men in Satan's army, to cast you into a furnace of fiery temptations, come not out of it till you are called; "let patience have its perfect work"; meekly keep your trying station till your heart is disengaged from all that is earthly, and till the sense of God's preserving power kindles in you such a faith in His omnipotent love as few experimentally know but they who have seen themselves like the mysterious bush in Horeb, burning, and yet unconsumed; or they who can say with St. Paul, "We are killed all the day long; and, behold, we live!"

Temptations," says Kempis, "are often very profitable to men, though they be troublesome and grievous: for in them a man is humbled, purified, and instructed. All the saints have passed through, and profited by, many tribulations; and they that could not bear temptations became reprobates, and fell away." "My son," adds the author of Ecclesiasticus (ii. 1-5), "if thou come to serve the Lord,"—"in the" perfect "beauty of holiness,"—"prepare thy soul for temptation. Set thy heart aright; constantly endure; and make not haste in the time of trouble. Whatever is brought upon thee take cheerfully, and be patient when thou art changed to a low estate. For gold is tried" and purified "in the fire, and acceptable men in the furnace of adversity." And therefore, says St. James, "Blessed is the man that endureth temptation; for, when he is tried," if he stands the fiery trial, "he shall receive the crown of life, which the Lord has promised to them that love Him"—with the love which "endureth" temptation and "all things," that is, with perfect love (James i. 12). Patiently endure, then, when God "for a season, if need be," will suffer you to "be in heaviness through manifold temptations." By this means, "the trial of your faith, being much more precious than that of gold which perisheth, though it be tried in the fire, will be found unto praise, and honour, and glory, at the appearing of Jesus Christ" (1 Pet. i. 7).

9. Deep repentance is good, gospel self-denial is excellent, and a degree of patient resignation in trials is of unspeakable use to attain the perfection of love;

but as "faith" immediately "works by love," it is of far more immediate use to purify the soul. Hence it is that Christ, the prophets, and the apostles so strongly insist upon faith; assuring us, that "if we will not believe, we shall not be established"; that "if we will believe, we shall see the glory of God," "we shall be saved," and the "rivers of living water shall flow from our inmost souls"; that "our hearts are purified by faith"; and that "we are saved by grace through faith." They tell us that "Christ gave Himself for the Church, that He might sanctify and cleanse it by the Word, that He might present it to Himself a glorious Church, not having spot, or wrinkle or any such thing," but that it should be "holy and without blemish." Now, if believers are to be cleansed and made without blemish by the Word, which testifies of the all-atoning blood, and the love of the Spirit, it is evident that they are to be sanctified by faith; for faith, or believing, has as necessary a reference to the Word as eating has to food. For the same reason the apostle observes, that "they who believe enter into rest"; that, "a promise being given us to enter in," we should "take care not to fall short of it through unbelief"; that we ought to take warning by the Israelites, who "could not enter" into the land of promise "through unbelief"; that we are "filled with all joy and peace in believing"; and that "Christ is able to save to the uttermost them who come unto

God through Him." Now, "coming," in the Scripture language, is another expression for believing: "He that cometh to God," says the apostle, "must believe." Hence it appears that faith is peculiarly necessary to those who will be "saved to the uttermost," especially a firm faith in the capital promise of the gospel of Christ, —the promise of "the Spirit of holiness," from the Father, through the Son. For "how shall they call on Him in whom they have not believed?" Or how can they earnestly plead the truth, and steadily wait for the performance, of a promise in which they have no faith? This doctrine of faith is supported by Peter's words: "God, who knoweth the hearts" of penitent believers, "bare them witness, giving them the Holy Ghost, and purifying their hearts by faith" (Acts xv. 8, 9). For the same Spirit of faith which initially purifies our hearts when we cordially believe the pardoning love of God, completely cleanses them, when we fully believe His sanctifying love.

10. This direction about faith being of the utmost importance, I shall confirm and explain it by an extract from Mr. Wesley's forty-third sermon, which points out "the Scripture way of salvation." "Though it be allowed," says this judicious divine, "that both this repentance and its fruits are necessary to full salvation, yet they are not necessary either in the same sense with faith, or in the same degree. Not in the same

degree; for these fruits are only necessary conditionally,—if there be time and opportunity for them; otherwise a man may be sanctified without them: but he cannot be sanctified without faith. Likewise, let a man have ever so much of this repentance, or ever so many good works, yet all this does not at all avail; he is not sanctified till he believes; but the moment he believes, with or without those fruits, yea, with more or less of this repentance, he is sanctified. Not in the same sense; for this repentance and these fruits are only remotely necessary— necessary in order to the continuance of his faith, as well as the increase of it; whereas faith is immediately and directly necessary to sanctification. It remains, that faith is the only condition which is immediately and proximately necessary to sanctification.

"But what is that faith whereby we are sanctified, saved from sin, and perfected in love? It is a divine evidence and conviction—(1) That God hath promised it in the Holy Scripture. Till we are thoroughly satisfied of this, there is no moving one step farther. And one would imagine there needed not one word more to satisfy reasonable man of this than the ancient promise: 'Then will I circumcise thy heart and the heart of thy seed, to love the Lord your God with all your heart and with all your soul.' How clearly does this express the being perfected in love! how strongly imply the being saved from all sin! For as long as love takes up the whole heart, what room is there for sin therein? (2) It is a divine evidence and conviction, that what God has promised He is able to perform. Admitting, therefore, that 'with men it is impossible' to bring 'a clean thing out of an unclean,' to purify the heart from all sin, and to fill it with all holiness, yet this creates no difficulty in the case, seeing 'with God all things are possible.' (3) It is an evidence and conviction, that He is able and willing to do it now. And why not? Is not a moment to Him the same as a thousand years? He cannot want more time to accomplish whatever is His will. We may therefore boldly say at any point of time, 'Now is the day of salvation. Behold, all things are now ready; come to the marriage.' (4) To this confidence—that God is both able and willing to sanctify us now—there needs to be added one thing more—a divine evidence and conviction that He doeth it. In that hour it is done. God says to the inmost soul, 'According to thy faith be it unto thee.' Then the soul is pure from every spot of sin, it is clean from all unrighteousness."

Those who have low ideas of faith will probably be surprised to see how much Mr. Wesley ascribes to that Christian grace; and to inquire why he so nearly connects our believing that God cleanses us from all sin, with God's actual cleansing of us from all sin. But their wonder will cease if they consider the definition which this divine gives of faith in the same sermon. "Faith in general," says he, "is defined by the apostle, an evidence, a divine evidence and conviction (the word used by the apostle means both), of things not seen, not visible, nor perceivable, either by sight or by any other of the external senses. It implies both a supernatural evidence of God and of the things of God; a kind of spiritual light exhibited to the soul, and a supernatural sight or perception thereof. Accordingly, the Scripture speaks of God's giving sometimes light, sometimes a power of discerning it. So St. Paul: 'God who commanded light to shine out of darkness, hath shined in our hearts; to give us the light of the knowledge of the glory of God in the face of Jesus Christ.' And elsewhere the same apostle speaks of 'the eyes of our understanding being opened.' By this twofold operation of the Holy Spirit, having the eyes of our souls both opened and enlightened, we see the things which the natural 'eye hath not seen, neither the ear heard.' We have a prospect of the invisible things of God: we see the spiritual world which is all round about us, and yet no more discerned by our natural faculties than if it had no being; and we see the eternal world piercing through the veil which hangs between time and eternity. Clouds and darkness then rest upon it no more, but we already see the glory which shall be revealed."

From this striking definition of faith it is evident that the doctrine of this address exactly coincides with Mr. Wesley's sermon, with this verbal difference only, that what he calls "faith implying a twofold operation of the Spirit, productive of spiritual light and supernatural sight," I have called "faith apprehending a sanctifying baptism, or outpouring, of the Spirit." His mode of expression savours more of the rational divine who logically divides the truth, in order to render its several parts conspicuous; and I keep closer to the words of the Scriptures, which, I hope, will frighten no candid Protestant. I make this remark for the sake of those who fancy, that when a doctrine is clothed with expressions which are not quite familiar to them it is a new doctrine, although these expressions should be as scriptural as those of a baptism or outpouring of the Spirit, which are used by some of the prophets, by John the Baptist, by the four evangelists, and by Christ Himself.

I have already pointed out the close connection there is between an act of faith which fully apprehends the sanctifying promise of the Father, and the power of the Spirit of Christ, which makes an end of moral corruption by forcing the lingering man of sin instantaneously to breathe out his last. Mr. Wesley, in the above-quoted sermon, touches upon this delicate subject in so clear and concise a manner, that while his discourse is before me, for the sake of those who have it not at hand, I shall transcribe the whole passage, and, by this means, put the seal of that eminent divine to what I have advanced in the preceding pages about sanctifying faith, and the quick destruction of sin.

"Does God work this great work in the soul gradually or instantaneously? Perhaps it may be gradually wrought in some, I mean in this sense,—they do not advert to the particular moment wherein sin ceases to be. But it is infinitely desirable, were it the will of God, that it should be done instantaneously, that the Lord should destroy sin 'by the breath of His mouth,' in a moment, in the twinkling of an eye. And so He generally does—a plain fact, of which there is evidence enough to satisfy any unprejudiced person. Thou therefore look for it every moment. Look for it in the way above described; in all those good works whereunto thou art created anew in Christ Jesus. There is then no danger; you can be no worse, if you are no better, for that expectation. For were you to be disappointed of your hope, still you lose nothing. But you shall not be disappointed of your hope; it will come, and will not tarry. Look for it then every day, every hour, every moment. Why not this hour, this moment? Certainly, you may look for it now if you believe it is by faith. And by this token you may surely know whether you seek it by faith or by works. If by works, you want something to be done first, before you are sanctified. You think, 'I must first be or do thus or thus.' Then you are seeking it by works unto this day. If you seek it by faith, you may expect it as you are; and if as you are, then expect it now. It is of importance to observe that there is an inseparable connection between these three points,—expect it by faith, expect it as you are, and expect it now. To deny one of them is to deny them all: to allow one is to allow them all. Do you believe we are sanctified by faith? Be true, then, to your principle, and look for this blessing just as you are, neither better nor worse, as a poor sinner that has still nothing to pay, nothing to plead, but 'Christ died.' And if you look for it as you are, then expect it now. Stay for nothing: why should you? Christ is ready, and He is all you want. He is waiting for you; He is at the door! Let your inmost soul cry out—

> 'Come in, come in, Thou heavenly guest!
> Nor hence again remove:
> But sup with me, and let the feast
> Be everlasting love.'"

11. Social prayer is closely connected with faith, in the capital promise of the sanctifying Spirit; and therefore I earnestly recommend that mean of grace, where it can be had, as being eminently conducive to the attaining of Christian perfection. When many believing hearts are lifted up, and wrestle with God in prayer together, you may compare them to many diligent hands which work a large machine. At such times, particularly, the fountains of the great deep are broken up, the windows of heaven are opened, and "rivers of living water flow" from the heart of obedient believers.

"In Christ when brethren join,
  And follow after peace,
The fellowship divine
  He promises to bless,
His chiefest graces to bestow
Where two or three are met below.

Where unity takes place,
  The joys of heaven we prove ;
This is the gospel grace,
  The unction from above,
The Spirit on all believers shed,
Descending swift from Christ their Head."

Accordingly we read that, when God powerfully opened the kingdom of the Holy Ghost on the day of Pentecost, the disciples "were all with one accord in one place." And when He confirmed that kingdom, they were lifting up "their voice to God with one accord" (see Acts ii. 1 and iv. 24). Thus also the believers at Samaria were filled with the Holy Ghost, the Sanctifier, while Peter and John prayed with them, and laid hands upon them.

12. But perhaps thou art alone. As a solitary bird, which sitteth on the housetop, thou lookest for a companion who may go with thee through the deepest travail of the regeneration. But, alas! thou lookest in vain ; all the professors about thee seem satisfied with their former experiences, and with self-imputed or self-conceited perfection. When thou givest them a hint of thy want of power from on high, and of thy hunger and thirst after a fulness of righteousness, they do not sympathise with thee. And, indeed, how can

they? "They are full" already, "they reign without thee, they have need of nothing." They do not sensibly want that "God would grant them, according to the riches of His glory, to be strengthened with might in the inner man, that Christ may dwell in their hearts by faith, that they, being rooted and grounded in love, may comprehend with all saints" perfected in love, "what is the breadth, and length, and depth, and height, and to know the love of Christ which passeth knowledge, that they might be filled with all the fulness of God" (Eph. iii. 16, etc.). They look upon thee as a whimsical person, full of singular notions; and they rather damp, than enliven, thy hopes. Thy circumstances are sad; but do not give place to despair, no, not for a moment. In the name of Christ, who could not get even Peter, James, and John to watch with Him one hour, and who was obliged to go through His agony alone; in His name, I say, "cast not away thy confidence, which has great recompence of reward." Under all thy discouragements, remember that, after all, divine grace is not confined to numbers, any more than to a few. When all outward helps fail thee, make the more of Christ, "on whom" sufficient "help is laid" for thee,—Christ, who says, "I will go with thee through fire and water"; the former "shall not burn thee, nor" the latter "drown thee." Jacob was alone when he wrestled with the angel, yet he prevailed; and if "the servant is not above his master," wonder not that it should be said of thee, as of thy Lord, when He went through His greatest temptations, "Of the people there was none with Him."

Should thy conflicts be "with confused noise, with burning, and fuel of fire"; should thy "Jerusalem be rebuilt in troublous times"; should the Lord "shake not the earth only, but also heaven"; should "deep call unto deep at the noise of His waterspouts"; should "all His waves and billows go over thee"; should thy patience be tried to the uttermost, remember how in years past thou hast tried the patience of God, nor be discouraged: an extremity and a storm are often God's opportunity. A blast of temptation, and a shaking of all thy foundations, may introduce the fulness of God to thy soul, and answer the end of the rushing wind, and of the shaking, which formerly accompanied the first great manifestations of the Spirit. The Jews still expect the coming of the Messiah in the flesh, and they particularly expect it in a storm. When lightnings flash, when thunders roar, when a strong wind shakes their houses, and the tempestuous sky seems to rush down in thunder-showers, then some of them particularly open their doors and windows to entertain their wished-for Deliverer. Do spiritually what they do carnally. Constantly wait for full "power from on high"; but especially when a storm of affliction, temptation, or distress overtakes thee; or when thy convictions and desires raise thee above thyself, as the waters of the flood raise Noah's ark above the earth; then be particularly careful to throw the door of faith and the window of hope as wide open as thou canst, and, spreading the arms of thy imperfect love, say with all the ardour and resignation which thou art master of—

> " My heart-strings groan with deep complaint,
> My flesh lies panting, Lord, for Thee;
> And every limb, and every joint,
> Stretches for perfect purity."

But if the Lord is pleased to come softly to thy help; if He makes an end of thy corruptions by helping thee gently to sink to unknown depths of meekness; if He drowns the indwelling man of sin by baptizing, by plunging him into an abyss of humility, do not find fault with the simplicity of His method, the plainness of His appearing, and the commonness of His prescription. Nature, like Naaman, is full of prejudices. She expects that Christ will come to make her clean with as much ado, pomp, and bustle as the Syrian general looked for when "he was wroth, and said, Behold, I thought, he will surely come out to me, and stand, and call on his God, and strike his hand over the place, and recover the leper." Christ frequently goes a much plainer way to work; and by this means He disconcerts all our preconceived notions and schemes of deliverance. "'Learn of Me to be meek and lowly in heart, and thou shalt find rest to thy soul,' the sweet rest of Christian perfection, of perfect humility, resignation, and meekness. Lie at My feet, as she did, who loved much, and was meekly taken up 'with the good part,' and 'the one thing needful.'" But thou frettest, thou despisest this robe of perfection, it is too plain for thee; thou slightest the "ornament of a meek and quiet spirit, which, in the sight of God, is of great price." Nothing will serve thy turn but a tawdry coat of many colours, which may please thy proud self-will, and draw the attention of others, by its glorious and flaming appearance: and it must be brought to thee with "lightnings, thunderings, and voices." If this is thy disposition, wonder not at the Divine wisdom which thinks fit to disappoint thy lofty prejudices; and let me address thee as Naaman's servants addressed him:— "My" brother, "if the prophet had bid thee do some great thing, wouldst thou not have done it? how much rather then, when he says to thee," "I am the meek and lowly Lamb of God," "wash" in the stream of My blood, plunge in the Jordan of My humility, "and be clean"? Instead therefore of going away from a plain Jesus in a rage, welcome Him in His lowest appearance, and be persuaded that He can as easily make an end of thy sin by gently coming in a still, small voice, as by rushing in upon thee in a storm, a fire, or an earthquake. The Jews rejected their Saviour, not so much because they did not earnestly desire His coming, as because He did not come in the manner in which they expected Him. It is probable that some of this Judaism cleaves to thee. If thou wilt absolutely come to Mount Sion in a triumphal chariot, or make thine entrance into the New Jerusalem upon a prancing horse, thou art likely never to come there. Leave, then, all thy lordly misconceptions behind; and humbly follow thy King, who makes His entry into the typical Jerusalem, "meek and lowly, riding upon an ass," yea, "upon a colt, the foal of an ass." I say it again, therefore, whilst thy faith and hope strongly insist on the blessing, let thy resignation and patience leave to God's infinite goodness and wisdom the peculiar manner of bestowing it. When He says, "Surely I come quickly" to "make My abode with thee," let thy faith close in with His word; ardently and yet meekly embrace His promise; it will instantly beget power, and with that power thou mayest instantly bring forth prayer, and possibly the prayer which opens heaven, humbly wrestles with God, inherits the blessing, and turns the well-known petition, "Amen! Even so, come, Lord Jesus," into the well-known praises, "He is come! He is come! Praise the Lord, O my soul," etc. Thus repent, believe, and obey; and "He that cometh, will come," with a fulness of pure, meek, humble love: "He will not tarry"; or, if He tarries, it will be to give to thy faith and desires more time to open, that thou mayest at His appearing be able to take in more of His perfecting grace and sanctifying power. Besides, thy expectation of His coming is of a purifying nature, and gradually sanctifies thee. "He that has this hope in him," by this very hope "purifies himself even as God is pure." For "we are saved" into perfect love "by hope," as well as "by faith." The "stalk" bears "the full corn in the ear," as well as the "root."

Up, then, thou sincere expectant of God's kingdom; let thy humble, ardent, free will meet prevenient, sanctifying, free grace in its weakest and darkest appearance, as the Father of the Faithful met the Lord, when He "appeared to him in the plain of Mamre" as a mere mortal: "Abraham lifted up his eyes, and looked; and, lo, three men stood by him": so does free grace, if I may venture upon the allusion, invite itself to thy tent; nay, it is now with thee in its creating, redeeming, and sanctifying influences. "And when he saw them, he ran to meet them from the tent door, and bowed himself towards the ground": "Go, and do likewise"; if thou seest any beauty in the humbling "grace of our Lord Jesus Christ," in the sanctifying "love of God," and in the comfortable "fellowship of the Holy Ghost," let thy free will "run to meet them, and bow itself toward the ground." Oh for a speedy going out of thy tent,—thy sinful self! Oh for a race of desire in the way of faith! Oh for incessant prostrations! Oh for a meek and deep bowing of thyself before thy divine Deliverer! "And Abraham said, My Lord, if now I have found favour in Thy sight, pass not away, I pray Thee, from Thy servant." Oh for the humble pressing of a loving faith! Oh for the faith which stopped the sun when God avenged His people in the days of Joshua! Oh for the importunate faith of the two disciples who detained Christ when "He made as though He would have gone farther!—They constrained Him, saying, Abide with us; for it is towards evening, and the day is far spent. And He went in to tarry with them." He soon, indeed, "vanished out of their" bodily "sight," because they were not called always to enjoy His bodily presence. Far from promising them that blessing, He had said, "It is expedient for you that I go away; for if I go not away, the Comforter will not come unto you; but if I depart, I will send Him unto you, that He may abide with you for ever. He dwelleth with you, and shall be in you." This promise is still "yea and amen in Christ": only plead it according to the preceding directions; and as sure as our Lord is "the true and faithful Witness," so sure will "the God of hope" and love soon "fill you with all joy and peace, that ye may abound in" pure love, as well as in confirmed "hope, through the power of the Holy Ghost." Then shall you have an indisputable right to join the believers who sing at the Tabernacle, and at the Lock Chapel—

> "Many are we now, and one,
> We who Jesus have put on:
> There is neither bond nor free,
> Male nor female, Lord, in Thee.

Love, like death, hath all destroy'd,
Render'd all distinctions void;
Names and sects, and parties fall;
Thou, O Christ, art All in all."

In the meantime you may sing, with the pious Countess of Huntingdon, the Rev. Mr. Madan, the Rev. Dr. Conyers, the Rev. Mr. Berridge, Richard Hill, Esq., and the imperfectionists who use their collections of hymns; ye may sing, I say, with them all, the two following hymns, which they have agreed to borrow from the hymns of Messrs. Wesley, after making some insignificant alterations. I transcribe them from the collection used in Lady Huntingdon's chapels, Bristol edition, 1765, page 239.

"O for a heart to praise my God,
A heart from sin set free,
A heart that's sprinkled with the blood
So freely spilt for me;

A heart resign'd, submissive, meek,
My dear Redeemer's throne,
Where only Christ is heard to speak,
Where Jesus reigns alone;

An humble, lowly, contrite heart,
Believing, true, and clean,
Which neither life nor death can part
From Him that dwells within;

A heart in every thought renew'd,
And fill'd with love divine,
Perfect, and right, and pure, and good,
A copy, Lord, of Thine!" etc.

"My heart, Thou knowest, can never rest
Till Thou create my peace;
Till, of mine Eden repossess'd,
From self and sin I cease.

> Thy nature, gracious Lord, impart ;
>   Come quickly from above ;
> Write Thy new name upon my heart,
>   Thy new, best name of love."

Here is undoubtedly an evangelical prayer for the love which restores the soul to a state of sinless rest and evangelical perfection. Mean ye, my brethren, what the good people who dissent from us print and sing, and I ask no more. Nor can ye wait for an answer to the prayer contained in the preceding hymn in a more scriptural manner, than by pleading the "promise of the Father" in such words as these—

> "Love divine, all love excelling,
>   Joy of heaven, to earth come down ;
> Fix in us Thine humble dwelling,
>   All Thy faithful mercies crown :
> Jesus, Thou art all compassion,
>   Pure, unbounded love Thou art !
> Visit us with Thy salvation,
>   Enter every trembling heart.
>
> Breathe, O breathe Thy loving Spirit
>   Into every troubled breast !
> Let us all in Thee inherit,
>   Let us find Thy promised rest : [1]
> Take away the power of sinning, [2]
>   Alpha and Omega be,
> End of faith as its beginning,
>   Set our hearts at liberty.

---

[1] Mr. Wesley says "second rest," because an imperfect believer enjoys a first, inferior rest : if he did not, he would be no believer.

[2] Is not this expression too strong ? Would it not be better to soften it as Mr. Hill has done, by saying "Take away the love of" (or

Come, Almighty, to deliver,
  Let us all Thy life receive;
Suddenly return, and never,
  Never more Thy temples leave:
Thee we would be always blessing,
  Serve Thee as Thine hosts above;
Pray, and praise Thee without ceasing,
  Glory in Thy precious love.

Finish then Thy new creation,
  Pure, unspotted, may we be;
Let us see Thy great salvation,
  Perfectly restored by Thee:
Changed from glory into glory,
  Till in heaven we take our place;
Till we cast our crowns before Thee,
  Lost in wonder, love, and praise."

Lift up your hands which hang down; our Aaron, our heavenly High Priest, is near to hold them up. The spiritual Amalekites will not always prevail; our Samuel, our heavenly prophet, is ready to cut them and their "king in pieces before the Lord." "The promise is unto you." You are surely called to attain the perfection of your dispensation, although you seem still afar off. Christ, in whom that perfection centres; Christ, from whom it flows, is very near, even at the door: "Behold," says He (and this He spake to Laodicean loiterers), "I stand at the door, and knock; if any man hear My voice, and open, I will come in, and sup with him," upon the fruits of My grace in their Christian perfection; and he "shall sup with Me," upon the fruits of My

the bent to) "sinning"? Can God take away from us our "power of sinning," without taking away our power of free obedience?

glory, in their angelical and heavenly maturity.

Hear this encouraging gospel: "Ask, and you shall have; seek, and you shall find; knock, and it shall be opened unto you. For every one that asketh, receiveth; and he that seeketh, findeth; and to him that knocketh, it shall be opened." "If any of you" believers "lack wisdom" (indwelling wisdom; "Christ, the wisdom and the power of God, dwelling in his heart by faith"), "let him ask of God, who giveth to all men, and upbraideth not; and it shall be given him. But let him ask" as a believer, "in faith, nothing wavering; for he that wavereth is like a wave of the sea, driven with the wind and tossed; for let not that man think that he shall receive the thing which he" thus "asketh." But "whatsoever things ye desire when ye pray, believe that ye receive them, and ye shall have them." For "all things" commanded and promised "are possible to him that believeth." He who has commanded us to be "perfect" in love "as our heavenly Father is perfect," and He who has promised "speedily to avenge His elect, who cry to Him night and day," He will speedily avenge you of your grand adversary, indwelling sin. He will say to you, "According to Thy faith be it done unto thee; for He is able to do far exceeding abundantly above all that we can ask or think"; and "of His fulness" we may "all receive grace for grace"; we may all witness the gracious fulfilment of all the promises which He has graciously made, "that by them we might be partakers of the divine nature," so far as it can be communicated to mortals in this world. You see that, with men, what you look for is impossible: but show yourselves believers; take God into the account, and you will soon experience that "with God all things are possible." Nor forget the omnipotent Advocate whom you have with Him. Behold, He lifts His once pierced hands, and says, "Father, sanctify them through Thy " loving " truth, that they may be perfected in one"; and, showing to you the Fountain of atoning blood, and purifying water, whence flow the streams which cleanse and gladden the heart of believers, He says, "Hitherto ye have asked nothing in My name; whatsoever ye shall ask the Father in My Name, He will give it you." "Ask," then, "that your joy may be full." If I try your faith by a little delay, if I hide My face for a moment, it is only to gather you with everlasting kindness. "A woman, when she is in travail, hath sorrow, because her hour is come; but as soon as she is delivered of the child, she remembereth no more the anguish for joy. Now ye have sorrow; but I will see you again, and your heart shall rejoice, and your joy no man taketh from you. In that day ye shall ask Me no question," for you shall not have My bodily presence; but My Urim and Thummim will be with you; and "the Spirit of truth will Himself lead you into all" Christian "truth."

> "O for a firm and lasting faith,
> To credit all the Almighty saith,
> To embrace the promise of His Son,
> And feel the Comforter our own."

In the meantime, be not afraid to "give glory to God" by believing in hope against hope. Stagger not at the "promise" of the Father and the Son, "through unbelief"; but trust the power and faithfulness of your Creator and Redeemer, till your Sanctifier has fixed His abode in your heart. Wait at mercy's door, as the lame beggar did at the "beautiful gate of the temple. Peter, fastening his eyes upon him, with John, said, Look on us: and he gave heed to them, expecting to receive something of them." Do so too; give heed to the Father in the Son, who says, "Look unto Me, and be ye saved." Expect to receive the "one thing" now "needful" for you,—a fulness of the sanctifying Spirit; and though your patience may be tried, it shall not be disappointed. The faith and power which, at Peter's word, gave the poor cripple a perfect soundness in the presence of all the wondering Jews, will give you at Christ's word a perfect soundness of heart, in the presence of all your adversaries.

> "Faith, mighty faith the promise sees,
> And looks to that alone,
> Laughs at impossibilities,
> And cries, It shall be done.
>
> Faith asks impossibilities;
> Impossibilities are given:
> And I, even I, from sin shall cease,
> Shall live on earth the life of heaven."

"Faith" always "works by love," by love of desire, at least, making us ardently pray for what we believe to be eminently desirable. And if Christian perfection appears so to you, you might, perhaps, express your earnest desire of it in some such words as these:—" How long, Lord, shall my soul, Thy spiritual temple, be a den of thieves, or a house of merchandise? How long shall vain thoughts profane it, as the buyers and sellers profaned Thy temple made with human hands? How long shall evil tempers lodge within me, how long shall unbelief, formality, hypocrisy, envy, hankering after sensual pleasure, indifference to spiritual delights, and backwardness to painful or ignominious duty, harbour there? How long shall these sheep and doves, yea, these goats and serpents, defile my breast, which should be pure as the holy of holies? how long shall they hinder me from being one of the worshippers whom Thou seekest— one of those who worship Thee in spirit and in truth? Oh, help me to take away these cages of unclean birds! 'Suddenly come to Thy temple.' Turn out all that offends the eye of Thy purity; and destroy all that keeps me out of 'the rest which remains for Thy' Christian 'people'; so shall I keep a spiritual Sabbath, a Christian jubilee to the God of my life; so shall I witness my share in the oil of joy with which Thou anointest perfect Christians above their fellow-believers. I stand in need of that oil, Lord: my lamp burns dim; sometimes it seems to be even gone out, as that of the foolish virgins: it is more like a 'smoking flax' than a 'burning and shining light.' Oh, quench it not; raise it to a flame. Thou knowest that I do believe in Thee. The trembling hand of my faith holds Thee; and though I have ten thousand times grieved Thy pardoning love, Thine everlasting arm is still under me, to redeem my life from destruction; while Thy right hand is over me, to crown me with mercies and lovingkindness. But, alas! I am neither sufficiently thankful for Thy present mercies, nor sufficiently athirst for Thy future favours; hence I feel an aching void in my soul, being conscious that I have not attained the heights of grace described in Thy word, and enjoyed by Thy holiest servants. Their deep experiences, the diligence and ardour with which they did Thy will, the patience and fortitude with which they endured the cross, reproach me, and convince me of my manifold wants. I want power from on high; I want the penetrating, lasting unction of the Holy One; I want to have my vessel—my capacious heart—full of the 'oil which maketh the countenance' of wise virgins 'cheerful'; I want a lamp of heavenly illumination, and a fire of divine love, burning day and night in my breast, as the typical lamps did in the temple, and the sacred fire on the altar; I want a full application of 'the blood which cleanses from all sin,' and a strong faith in Thy sanctifying Word—a faith by which Thou mayest dwell in my heart, as the unwavering hope of glory, and the fixed object of my love; I want the internal oracle,—Thy 'still, small voice,'—together with Urim and Thummim,[1]—'the new name which none knoweth but he that receiveth it': in a word, Lord, I want a plenitude of Thy Spirit, the full promise of the Father, and the rivers which flow from the inmost soul of the believers who have gone on to the perfection of Thy dispensation. I do believe that Thou canst and wilt thus 'baptize me with the Holy Ghost, and with fire.'. Help my unbelief; confirm and increase my faith with regard to this important baptism. 'Lord, I have need to be' thus 'baptized of Thee,' and 'I am straitened till this baptism is accomplished.' By Thy baptism of tears in the manger, of water in Jordan, of sweat in Gethsemane, 'of blood, and fire, and vapour of smoke,' and flaming wrath on Calvary,—baptize, O baptize my soul, and make as full an end of the original sin which I have from Adam, as Thy last baptism made of the 'likeness of sinful flesh' which Thou hadst from a daughter of Eve. Some of Thy people look at death for full salvation from sin; but at Thy command, Lord, I look unto Thee. Say to my soul, 'I am thy salvation'; and let me feel in my heart, as well as see with my understanding, that Thou canst 'save' from sin 'to the uttermost all that come to God through Thee.' I am tired of forms, professions, and orthodox notions, so far as they are not pipes or channels to

[1] Two Hebrew words, which mean "lights" and "perfections."

convey life, light, and love to my dead, dark, and stony heart. Neither the plain letter of Thy gospel, nor the sweet foretastes and transient illuminations of Thy Spirit, can satisfy the large desires of my faith. Give me Thine abiding Spirit, that He may continually shed abroad Thy love in my soul. Come, O Lord, with that blessed Spirit; come, Thou and Thy Father, in that Holy Comforter; come to make your abode with me; or I shall go meekly mourning to my grave. Blessed mourning! Lord, increase it. I had rather wait in tears for Thy fulness, than wantonly waste the fragments of Thy spiritual bounties, or feed with Laodicean contentment upon the tainted manna of my former experiences. Righteous Father, I hunger and thirst after Thy righteousness: send Thy Holy Spirit of promise, to fill me therewith, to sanctify me throughout, and to seal me centrally to the day of eternal redemption, and finished salvation. 'Not for works of righteousness which I have done, but of Thy mercy,' for Christ's sake, 'save Thou me by the' complete 'washing of regeneration, and the' full 'renewing of the Holy Ghost'; and in order to this, pour out of Thy Spirit, shed it abundantly on me, till the fountain of living water abundantly springs up in my soul, and I can say, in the full sense of the words, that 'Thou livest in me,' that 'my life is hid with Thee in God,' and that 'my spirit is returned to Him that gave it,'—to Thee, the first and the last, my author and my end, my God and my all."

YE have not sung the preceding hymns in vain, O ye men of God, who have mixed faith with your evangelical requests. The God who says, "Open thy mouth wide and I will fill it"; the gracious God who declares, "Blessed are they that hunger after righteousness, for they shall be filled,"—that faithful, covenant-keeping God has now "filled you with all righteousness, peace, and joy in believing." The brightness of Christ's appearing has destroyed the indwelling man of sin. He who had slain the lion and the bear, He who had already done so great things for you, has now crowned all His blessings by slaying the Goliath within. Aspiring, unbelieving self is fallen before the victorious Son of David. The "quick and powerful word of God," which is "sharper than any two-edged sword," has "pierced even to the dividing asunder of soul and spirit." The carnal mind is cut off; "the circumcision of the heart, through the Spirit," has fully taken place in your breasts; and now "that mind is in you which was also in Christ Jesus"; ye are spiritually-minded; loving God with all your heart, and your neighbour as yourselves, ye are full of goodness, ye keep the commandments, ye observe "the law of liberty," ye "fulfil the law of Christ. Of Him" ye have "learned to be meek and lowly in heart." Ye have fully "taken His yoke upon you"; in so doing, ye have "found" a sweet abiding "rest unto your souls"; and from blessed experience ye can say, "Christ's yoke is easy, and His burden is light"; His "ways are ways of pleasantness, and all His paths are peace"; "all the paths of the Lord are mercy and truth, unto such as keep His covenant and His testimonies." The beatitudes are sensibly yours; and the charity described by St. Paul has the same place in your breasts which the tables of the law had in the ark of the covenant. Ye are the living temples of the Trinity; the Father is your life, the Son your light, the Spirit your love; ye are truly baptized into the mystery of God, ye continue to "drink into one Spirit," and thus ye enjoy the grace of both sacraments. There is an end of your "lo here!" and "lo there!" "The kingdom of God is" now established "within you." Christ's "righteousness, peace, and joy" are rooted in your breasts "by the Holy Ghost given unto you," as an abiding guide and indwelling Comforter. Your introverted eye of faith looks at God, who gently "guides you with His eye into all the truth" necessary to make you "do justice, love mercy, and walk humbly with your God." Simplicity of intention keeps darkness out of your mind, and purity of affection keeps wrong fires out of your breast. By the former ye are without guile; by the latter ye are without envy. Your passive will instantly melts into the will of God; and on all occasions you meekly say, "Not my will, O Father, but Thine be done": thus are ye always ready to suffer what you are called to suffer. Your active will evermore says, "Speak, Lord, Thy servant heareth: what wouldest Thou have me to do? It is my meat and drink to do the will of my heavenly Father"; thus are ye always ready to do whatsoever ye are convinced that God calls you to do; and "whatsoever ye do, whether ye eat, or drink, or do anything else, ye do all to the glory of God, and in the name of our Lord Jesus Christ; rejoicing evermore; praying without ceasing; in everything giving thanks"; solemnly "looking for, and hasting unto," the hour of your dissolution, and "the day of God, wherein the heavens being on fire shall be dissolved," and your soul, being clothed with a celestial body, shall be able to do celestial services to the God of your life.

In this blessed state of Christian perfection, the holy "anointing which ye have received of Him abideth in you, and ye need not that any man teach you, unless it be as the same anointing teacheth." Agreeably, therefore, to that anointing, which teaches by a variety of means, which formerly taught a prophet by an ass, and daily instructs God's children by the ant, I shall venture to set before you some important directions, which the Holy Ghost has already suggested to your pure minds: for "I would not be negligent to put you in remembrance of these things, though ye know them, and be established in the present truth. Yea, I think it meet to stir you up by putting you in remembrance," and giving you some hints, which it is safe for you frequently to meditate upon.

I. Adam, ye know, lost his human perfection in paradise; Satan lost his angelic perfection in heaven; the devil thrust sore at Christ in the wilderness, to throw Him down from His mediatorial perfection; and St. Paul, in the same epistles where he professes not only Christian but apostolic perfection also (Phil. iii. 15; 1 Cor. i. 6; 2 Cor. xii. 11), informs us that he continued to "run for the crown of heavenly" perfection like a man who might not only lose his crown of Christian perfection, but become a reprobate, and be cast away (1 Cor. ix. 25–27). And therefore so run ye also, "that no man take your crown" of Christian perfection in this world, and "that ye may obtain" your crown of angelic perfection in the world to come. Still keep your body under. Still guard your senses. Still watch your own heart; and "steadfast in the faith," still "resist the devil," that he may "flee from you"; remembering, that if Christ Himself, as Son of Man, had "conferred with flesh and blood," refused to deny Himself, and avoided taking up His cross, He had lost His perfection, and sealed up our original apostasy.

"We do not find," says Mr. Wesley, in his *Plain Account of Christian Perfection*, "any general state described in Scripture from which a man cannot draw back to sin. If there were any state wherein this was impossible, it would be that of those who are sanctified, who are fathers in Christ, who 'rejoice evermore, pray without ceasing, and in everything give thanks.' But it is not impossible for these to draw back. They who are sanctified may yet fall and perish (Heb. x. 29). Even fathers in Christ need that warning, 'Love not the world' (1 John ii. 15). They who 'rejoice, pray, and give thanks, without ceasing,' may, nevertheless, 'quench the Spirit' (1 Thess. v. 16, etc.). Nay, even they who are 'sealed unto the day of redemption' may yet 'grieve the Holy Spirit of God' (Eph. iv. 30)."

The doctrine of the absolute perseverance of the saints is the first card which the devil played against man : "'Ye shall not surely die,' if ye break the law of your perfection." This fatal card won the game. Mankind and paradise were lost. The artful serpent had too well succeeded at his first game, to forget that lucky card at his second. See him "transforming himself into an angel of light" on the pinnacle of the temple. There he plays over again his old game against the Son of God. Out of the Bible he pulls the very card which won our first parents, and swept the stake—Paradise ; yea, swept it with the besom of destruction. "Cast Thyself down," says he ; "for it is written," that all things shall work together for Thy good, Thy very falls not excepted : "He shall give His angels charge concerning Thee, and in their hands they shall bear Thee up, lest at any time Thou dash Thy foot against a stone." The tempter, thanks be to Christ, lost the game at that time; but he did not lose his card; and it is probable that he will play it round against you all, only with some variation. Let me mention one among a thousand. He promised our Lord that God's angels should bear Him up in their hands, if He threw Himself down; and it is not unlikely that he will promise you greater things still. Nor should I wonder if he was bold enough to hint, that, when you cast yourselves down, God Himself shall bear you up in His hands, yea in His arms of everlasting love. Oh, ye men of God, learn wisdom by the fall of Adam. Oh, ye anointed sons of the Most High, learn watchfulness by the conduct of Christ. If He was afraid to "tempt the Lord His God," will ye dare to do it? If He rejected as poison the hook of the absolute perseverance of the saints, though it was baited with Scripture, will ye swallow it down, as if it were "honey out of the Rock of Ages"? No: "through faith in Christ the Scriptures have made you wise unto salvation"; you will not only fly with all speed from evil, but from the very appearance of evil. And when you stand on the brink of a temptation, far from entering into it, under any pretence whatever, ye will leap back into the bosom of Him who says, "Watch and pray, lest ye enter into temptation; for" though "the spirit is willing, the flesh is weak." I grant that, evangelically speaking, the weakness of the flesh is not sin; but yet the "deceitfulness of sin" creeps in at this door; and by this means not a few of God's children, "after they had escaped the pollutions of the world, through the" sanctifying "knowledge of Christ," under plausible pretences, "have been again entangled therein and overcome." Let their falls make you cautious. Ye have put on the whole armour of God: Oh, keep it on, and use it "with all prayer," that ye may, to the last, "stand complete in Christ," and be "more than conquerors" through Him that has loved you.

II. Remember that "every one who is perfect shall be as his Master." Now, if your Master was tempted and assaulted to the last; if to the last He watched and prayed, using all the means of grace Himself, and enforcing the use of them upon others; if to the last He fought against the world, the flesh, and the devil, and did not "put off the harness" till He had put off the body, think not yourselves above Him, but "go and do likewise." If He did not regain paradise, without going through the most complete renunciation of all the good things of this world, and without meekly submitting to the severe stroke of His last enemy, death, be content to be "perfect as He was"; nor fancy that your flesh and blood can inherit the celestial kingdom of God, when the flesh and blood which Emmanuel Himself assumed from a pure virgin could not inherit it without passing under the cherub's flaming sword; I mean, without going through the gates of death.

III. Ye are not complete in wisdom. Perfect love does not imply perfect knowledge; but perfect humility, and perfect readiness to receive instruction. Remember, therefore, that if ever ye show that ye are above being instructed, even by a fisherman who teaches according to the Divine anointing, ye will show that ye are fallen from a perfection of humility into a perfection of pride.

IV. Do not confound angelical with Christian perfection. Uninterrupted transports of praise, and ceaseless raptures of joy, do not belong to Christian but to angelical perfection. Our feeble frame can bear but a few drops of that glorious cup. In general, that "new wine" is too strong for our "old bottles"; that power is too excellent for our earthen cracked vessels; but, weak as they are, they can bear a fulness of meekness, of resignation, of humility, and of that love which is willing to obey unto death. If God indulges you with ecstasies and extraordinary revelations, be thankful for them, but be "not exalted above measure by them"; take care lest enthusiastic delusions mix themselves with them; and remember that your Christian perfection does not so much consist in "building a tabernacle" upon Mount Tabor, to rest and enjoy rare sights there, as in resolutely taking up the cross, and following Christ to the palace of a proud Caiaphas, to the judgment-hall of an unjust Pilate, and to the top of an ignominious Calvary. Ye never read in your Bibles, "Let that glory be upon you, which was also upon St. Stephen, when 'he looked up steadfastly into heaven, and said, Behold, I see the heavens opened, and the Son of Man standing on the right hand of God.'" But ye have frequently read there, "Let this mind be in you, which was also in Christ Jesus, who made Himself of no reputation, took upon Him the form of a servant, and, being found in fashion as a man, humbled Himself, and became obedient unto death, even the death of the cross."

See Him on that ignominious gibbet: He hangs, abandoned by His friends, surrounded by His foes, condemned by the rich, insulted by the poor. He hangs, a worm, and no man! a very scorn of men, and the outcast of the people! "All they that see Him laugh Him to scorn. They shoot out their lips and shake their heads, saying, He trusted in God that He would deliver Him; let Him deliver Him, if He will have Him." "There is none to help Him." One of His apostles denies, another sells Him, and the rest run away. "Many oxen are come about Him; fat bulls of Bashan close Him on every side; they gape upon Him with their mouths, as it were a ramping lion. He is poured out like water; His heart in the midst of His body is like melting wax; His strength is dried up like a potsherd; His tongue cleaveth to His gums; He is going into the dust of death. Many dogs are come about Him, and the counsel of the wicked layeth siege against Him. His hands and feet are pierced. You may tell all his bones. They stand staring and looking upon Him. They part His garments among them, and cast lots" for the only remain of His property, His plain, seamless vesture. Both suns, the visible and the invisible, seem eclipsed. No cheering beam of created light gilds His gloomy prospect. No smile of His heavenly Father supports His agonising soul. No cordial, unless it be vinegar and gall, revives His sinking spirits. He has nothing left, except His God. But His God is enough for Him. In His God He has all things. And though His soul is "seized with sorrow, even unto death," yet it hangs more firmly upon His God by a naked faith, than His lacerated body does on the cross by the clinched nails. The perfection of His love shines in all its Christian glory. He not only forgives His insulting foes and bloody persecutors, but in the highest point of His passion He forgets His own wants, and thirsts after their eternal happiness. Together with His blood, He pours out His soul for them; and, excusing them all, He says, "Father, forgive them, for they know not what they do." Oh, ye adult sons of God, "in" this "glass behold all with open face the glory" of your

Redeemer's forgiving, praying love; and, as ye behold it, "be changed into the same image from glory to glory, by the loving Spirit of the Lord."

V. This lesson is deep; but He may teach you one deeper still: by a strong sympathy with Him in all His sufferings He may call you to know Him every way crucified. Stern justice thunders from heaven, "Awake, O sword, against the man who is My fellow!" The sword awakes, the sword goes through His soul, the flaming sword is quenched in His blood. But is one sinew of His perfect faith cut, one fibre of His perfect resignation injured, by the astonishing blow? No: His God slays Him, and yet He trusts in His God. By the noblest of all ventures, in the most dreadful of all storms, He meekly bows His head, and shelters His departing soul in the bosom of His God: "My God! My God!" says He, "though all Thy comforts have forsaken Me, and all Thy storms and waves go over Me, yet into Thy hands I commend My spirit." "For Thou wilt not leave My soul in hell, neither wilt Thou suffer Thine Holy One to see corruption. Thou wilt show Me the path of life: in Thy presence is fulness of joy, and at Thy right hand," where I shall soon sit, "there are pleasures for evermore." What a pattern of perfect confidence! Oh, ye perfect Christians, be ambitious to ascend to those amazing heights of Christ's perfection; "for even hereunto were ye called, because Christ also suffered for us, leaving us an example, that ye should follow His steps; who knew no sin; who, when He was reviled, reviled not again; when He suffered, He threatened not, but committed Himself to Him that judgeth righteously." If this is your high calling on earth, rest not, oh ye fathers in Christ, till your patient hope and perfect confidence in God have got their last victory over your last enemy —the king of terrors.

"The ground of a thousand mistakes," says Mr. Wesley, "is, the not considering deeply that love is the highest gift of God, humble, gentle, patient love; that all visions, revelations, manifestations whatever, are little things compared to love. It were well you should be thoroughly sensible of this: the heaven of heavens is love. There is nothing higher in religion; there is, in effect, nothing else. If you look for anything but more love, you are looking wide of the mark, you are getting out of the royal way. And when you are asking others, 'Have you received this or that blessing?' if you mean anything but more love, you mean wrong; you are leading them out of the way, and putting them upon a false scent. Settle it, then, in your heart, that, from the moment God has saved you from all sin, you are to aim at nothing but more of that love described in 1 Cor. xiii. You can go no higher than this, till you are carried into Abraham's bosom."

VI. Love is humble: "Be therefore clothed with humility," says Mr. Wesley; "let it not only fill but cover you all over. Let modesty and self-diffidence appear in all your words and actions. Let all you speak and do show that you are little, and base, and mean, and vile in your own eyes. As one instance of this, be always ready to own any fault you have been in: if you have at any time thought, spoke, or acted wrong, be not backward to acknowledge it; never dream that this will hurt the cause of God: no; it will further it. Be therefore open and frank when you are taxed with anything: let it appear just as it is; and you will thereby not hinder, but adorn, the gospel." Why should ye be more backward in acknowledging your failings, than in confessing that ye do not pretend to infallibility? St. Paul was perfect in the love which casts out fear, and therefore he boldly reproved the high priest. But when he had reproved him more sharply than the fifth commandment allows, he directly confessed his mistake, and set his seal to the importance of the duty in which he had been inadvertently wanting: "Then Paul said, I knew not, brethren, that he was the high priest: for it is written, Thou shalt not speak evil of the ruler of thy people." St. John was perfect in the courteous, humble love which brings us down at the feet of all. His courtesy, his humility, and the dazzling glory which beamed forth from a divine messenger, whom he apprehended to be more than a creature, betrayed him into a fault contrary to that of St. Paul; but, far from concealing it, he openly confessed it, and published his confession for the edification of all the churches. "When I had heard and seen," says he, "I fell down to worship before the feet of the angel who showed me these things. Then saith he unto me, See thou do it not; for I am thy fellow-servant." Christian perfection shines as much in the childlike simplicity with which the perfect readily acknowledge their faults, as it does in the manly steadiness with which they "resist unto blood, striving against sin."

VII. If humble love makes us frankly confess our faults, much more does it incline us to own ourselves sinners, miserable sinners, before that God whom we have so frequently offended. I need not remind you that your "bodies are dead because of sin"; you see, you feel it: and therefore, so long as you dwell in a prison of flesh and blood, which death the revenger of sin is to pull down; so long as your final justification, as pardoned and sanctified sinners, has not taken place; yea, so long as you break the law of paradisiacal perfection, under which you were originally placed, it is meet, right, and your bounden duty to consider yourselves as sinners, who, as transgressors of the law of innocence and the law of liberty, are guilty of death, of eternal death. St. Paul did so, after he was "come to Mount Sion and to the spirits of just men made perfect": he still looked upon himself as the "chief of sinners," because he had been a daring blasphemer of Christ, and a fierce persecutor of His people: "Christ," says he, "came to save sinners, of whom I am chief." The reason is plain. Matter of fact is, and will be, matter of fact to all eternity. According to the doctrines of grace and justice, and before the throne of God's mercy and holiness, a sinner pardoned and sanctified must, in the very nature of things, be considered as a sinner; for if you consider him as a saint, absolutely abstracted from the character of a sinner, how can he be a pardoned and sanctified sinner? To all eternity, therefore, but much more while "death, the wages of sin," is at your heels, and while ye are going to "appear before the judgment-seat of Christ," to receive your final sentence of absolution or condemnation, it will become you to say with St. Paul, "We have all sinned, and come short of the glory of God; being justified freely," as sinners, "by His grace, through the redemption that is in Jesus Christ"; —although we are justified judicially; as believers, through faith; as obedient believers, through the obedience of faith; and as perfect Christians, through Christian perfection.

VIII. Humble love "becomes all things," but sin, "to all men," although it delights most in those who are most holy. Ye may, and ought to, set your love of peculiar complacence upon God's dearest children, upon those who, like yourselves, excel in virtue; because they more strongly reflect the image of the God of love, the Holy One of Israel. But if ye despise the weak, and are above lending them a helping hand, ye are fallen from Christian perfection, which teaches us to "bear one another's burdens," especially the burdens of the weak. Imitate, then, the tenderness and wisdom of the Good Shepherd, who "carries the lambs in His bosom, gently leads the sheep which are big with young," feeds with milk those who cannot bear strong meat, and says to His imperfect disciples, "I have many things to say to you, but ye cannot bear them now."

IX. "Where the loving Spirit of the Lord is, there is liberty"; keep therefore at the utmost distance from the shackles of a narrow, prejudiced, bigoted spirit. The moment ye confine your love to the people who think just as you do, and your regard to the preachers who exactly suit your taste, you fall from perfection, and turn bigots. "I entreat you," says Mr. Wesley, in his *Plain Account*, "beware of bigotry. Let not your love or beneficence be confined to Methodists (so called) only; much less to that very small part of them who seem to be renewed in love, or to those who believe yours and their report. Oh, make not this your 'shibboleth.'" On the contrary, as ye have time and ability, "do good to all men." Let your benevolence shine upon all; let your charity send its cherishing beams towards all, in proper degrees; so shall ye be "perfect as your heavenly Father," who "makes His sun to shine upon all," although He sends the brightest and warmest beams of His favour upon the household of faith, and reserves His richest bounties for those who lay out their five talents to the best advantage.

X. Love, pure love, is satisfied with the supreme Good, with God. "Beware, then, of desiring anything but Him. Now you desire nothing else: every other desire is driven out; see that none enter in again. Keep thyself pure: let 'your eye remain single, and your whole body shall be full of light.' Admit no desire of pleasing food, or any other pleasure of sense; no desire of pleasing the eye, or the imagination; no desire of money, of praise, or esteem; of happiness in any creature. You may bring these desires back, but you need not: you may feel them no more. Oh, 'stand fast in the liberty wherewith Christ hath made you free.' Be patterns to all of denying yourselves, and taking up your cross daily. Let them see that you make no account of any pleasure which does not bring you nearer to God, nor regard any pain which does; that you simply aim at pleasing Him, whether by doing or suffering; that the constant language of your heart, with regard to pleasure or pain, honour or dishonour, riches or poverty, is—

> 'All's alike to me, so I
> In my Lord may live and die.'"

XI. The best soldiers are sent upon the most difficult and dangerous expeditions; and as you are the best soldiers of Jesus Christ, ye will probably be called to drink deepest of His cup, and to carry the heaviest burdens. "Expect contradiction and opposition," says the judicious divine whom I have just quoted, "together with crosses of various kinds. Consider the words of St. Paul: 'To you it is given in the behalf of Christ,' for His sake, as a fruit of His death and intercession for you, 'not only to believe, but also to suffer for His sake' (Philip. i. 29). 'It is given' —God gives you this opposition or reproach; it is a fresh token of His love. And will you disown the giver? or spurn His gift, and count it a misfortune? Will you not rather say, 'Father, the hour is come, that Thou shouldest be glorified. Now Thou givest Thy child to suffer something for Thee. Do with me according to Thy will.' Know that these things, far from being hindrances to the work of God, or to your soul, unless by your own fault, are not only unavoidable in the course of providence, but profitable, yea necessary, for you; therefore, receive them from God, not from chance, with willingness, with thankfulness; receive them from men with humility, meekness, yieldingness, gentleness, sweetness."

Love can never do nor suffer too much for its Divine Object. Be then ambitious, like St. Paul, to be made perfect in sufferings. I have already observed that the apostle, not satisfied to be a perfect Christian, would also be a perfect martyr, earnestly desiring to "know the fellowship of Christ's" utmost "sufferings." Follow him, as he followed his suffering, crucified Lord. "Your feet are shod with the preparation of the gospel of peace": run after them both in the race of obedience, for the crown of martyrdom, if that crown is reserved for you. And if ye miss the crown of those who are martyrs in deed, ye shall, however, receive the reward of those who are martyrs in intention—the crown of righteousness and angelical perfection.

XII. But do not so desire to follow Christ to the garden of Gethsemane, as to refuse following Him now to the carpenter's shop, if Providence now calls you to it. Do not lose the present day by idly looking back at yesterday, or foolishly antedating the cares of to-morrow; but wisely use every hour, spending them as one who stands on the verge of time, on the border of eternity, and who has his work cut out by a wise Providence from moment to moment. Never, therefore, neglect using the two talents you have now, and doing the duty which is now incumbent upon you. Should ye be tempted to it under the plausible pretence of waiting for a greater number of talents, remember that God doubles our talents in the way of duty, and that it is a maxim advanced by Elisha Coles himself, "Use grace, and have" more "grace." Therefore, "to continual watchfulness and prayer, add continual employment," says Mr. Wesley; "for grace flies a vacuum, as well as nature; the devil fills whatever God does not fill." "As 'by works faith is made perfect,' so the completing or destroying the work of faith, and enjoying the favour or suffering the displeasure of God, greatly depends on every single act of obedience." If you forget this, you will hardly do now whatsoever your hand findeth to do. Much less will you do it with all your might for God, for eternity.

XIII. Love is modest; it rather inclines to bashfulness and silence than to talkative forwardness. "In a multitude of words there wanteth not sin": "be," therefore, "slow to speak"; "nor cast your pearls before" those who cannot distinguish them from pebbles. Nevertheless, when you are solemnly called upon to bear testimony to the truth, and to say what great things God has done for you, it would be cowardice, or false prudence, not to do it with humility. "Be," then, "always ready to give an answer to every man who" properly "asketh you a reason of the hope that is in you, with meekness," without fluttering anxiety, "and with fear," with a reverential awe of God upon your minds (1 Peter iii. 15). The perfect are "burning and shining lights";

and our Lord intimates that, as "a candle is not lighted to be put under a bushel, but upon a candlestick, that it may give light to all the house," so God does not light the candle of perfect love to hide it in a corner, but to give light to all those who are within the reach of its brightness. If diamonds glitter, if stars shine, if flowers display their colours, and perfumes diffuse their fragrance, to the honour of the Father of lights, and Author of every good gift, if, without self-seeking, they disclose His glory to the utmost of their power, why should ye not "go and do likewise"? Gold answers its most valuable end, when it is brought to light, and made to circulate for charitable and pious uses; and not when it lies concealed in a miser's strong box, or in the dark bosom of a mine. But when you lay out your spiritual gold for proper uses, beware of imitating the vanity of those coxcombs who, as often as they are about to pay for a trifle, pull out a handful of gold, merely to make a show of their wealth.

XIV. Love, or "charity, rejoiceth in the" display of an edifying "truth." Fact is fact all the world over. If you can say to the glory of God, that you are alive, and feel very well when you do so, why could you not also testify to His honour, that you live not, but that Christ liveth in you, if you really find that this is your experience? Did not St. John say, "Our love is made perfect, because, as He is, so are we in this world"? Did not St. Paul write, "The righteousness of the law is fulfilled in us, who walk after the Spirit"? Did he not with the same simplicity aver that, although he "had nothing," and was "sorrowful," yet he "possessed all things," and was "always rejoicing"?

Hence it appears that, with respect to the declaring or concealing what God has done for your soul, the line of your duty runs exactly between the proud forwardness of some stiff pharisees and the voluntary humility of some stiff mystics. The former vainly boast of more than they experience; and by that means they set up the cursed idol, self: the latter ungratefully hide the wonderful works of God, which the primitive Christians spoke of publicly in a variety of languages; and by this means they refuse to exalt their gracious benefactor, Christ. The first error is undoubtedly more odious than the second; but what need is there of leaning to either? Would ye avoid them both? Let your tempers and lives always declare that perfect love is attainable in this life; and when you have a proper call to declare it with your lips and pens, do it without forwardness, to the glory of God; do it with simplicity, for the edification of your neighbour; do it with godly jealousy, lest ye should show the treasures of Divine grace in your hearts, with the same self-complacence with which King Hezekiah showed his treasures, and the golden vessels of the temple, to the ambassadors of the King of Babylon, remembering what a dreadful curse this piece of vanity pulled down upon him: "And Isaiah said unto Hezekiah, Hear the word of the Lord: Behold, the days come, that all that is in thine house shall be carried into Babylon; nothing shall be left, saith the Lord." If God so severely punished Hezekiah's pride, how properly does St. Peter charge believers to give with fear an account of the grace which is in them! and how careful should ye be to observe this important charge!

XV. If you will keep at the utmost distance from the vanity which proved so fatal to good King Hezekiah, follow an excellent direction of Mr. Wesley. When you have done anything for God, or "received any favour from Him, retire, if not into your closet, into your heart, and say, 'I come, Lord, to restore to Thee what Thou hast given, and I freely relinquish it, to enter again into my own nothingness. For what is the most perfect creature in heaven or earth in Thy presence, but a void, capable of being filled with Thee and by Thee, as the air which is void and dark is capable of being filled with the light of the sun? Grant therefore, O Lord, that I may never appropriate Thy grace to myself, any more than the air appropriates to itself the light of the sun, who withdraws it every day to restore it the next; there being nothing in the air that either appropriates His light or resists it. Oh, give me the same facility of receiving and restoring Thy grace and good works! I say, Thine; for I acknowledge that the root from which they spring is in Thee, and not in me.' The true means to be filled anew with the riches of grace is thus to strip ourselves of it: without this it is extremely difficult not to faint in the practice of good works." "And therefore, that your good works may receive their last perfection, let them lose themselves in God. This is a kind of death to them, resembling that of our bodies, which will not attain their highest life, their immortality, till they lose themselves in the glory of our souls, or rather of God, wherewith they shall be filled. And it is only what they had of earthly and mortal which good works lose by this spiritual death."

XVI. Would ye see this deep precept put in practice? Consider St. Paul. Already possessed of Christian perfection, he does good works from morning till night. He "warns every one night and day with tears." He carries the gospel from east to west. Wherever he stops, he plants a church at the hazard of his life. But instead of resting in his present perfection, and in the good works which spring from it, "he grows in grace and in the knowledge of our Lord Jesus Christ"; unweariedly "following after, if that he may apprehend that" perfection "for which also he is apprehended of Christ Jesus," that celestial perfection of which he got lively ideas when he was "caught up to the third heaven, and heard unspeakable words, which is not lawful for a man to utter." With what amazing ardour does he run his race of Christian perfection for the prize of that higher perfection! How does he forget the works of yesterday, when he lays himself out for God to-day! "Though dead, he yet speaketh"; nor can an address to perfect Christians be closed by a more proper speech than his. "Brethren," says he, "be followers of me." "I count not myself to have apprehended" my angelical perfection; "but this one thing I do, forgetting those things which are behind," settling in none of my former experiences, resting in none of my good works, "and, reaching forth unto those things which are before, I press towards the mark, for the" celestial "prize of the high calling of God in Christ Jesus. Let us therefore, as many as are perfect, be thus minded; and if in anything ye be otherwise minded, God shall reveal even this unto you." In the meantime you may sing the following hymn of the Rev. Mr. Charles Wesley, which is descriptive of the destruction of corrupt self-will, and expressive of the absolute resignation which characterises a perfect believer:—

> " To do or not to do; to have
>   Or not to have, I leave to Thee;
> To be or not to be, I leave:
>   Thy only will be done in me.
> All my requests are lost in one:
> Father, Thy only will be done.

Suffice that, for the season past,
  Myself in things divine I sought,
For comforts cried with eager haste,
  And murmur'd that I found them not.
I leave it now to Thee alone :
Father, Thy only will be done.

Thy gifts I clamour for no more,
  Or selfishly Thy grace require,
An evil heart to varnish o'er ;
  Jesus, the Giver, I desire ;
After the flesh no longer known :
Father, Thy only will be done.

Welcome alike the crown or cross ;
  Trouble I cannot ask, nor peace,
Nor toil, nor rest, nor gain, nor loss,
  Nor joy, nor grief, nor pain, nor ease,
Nor life, nor death ; but ever groan,
Father, Thy only will be done."

This hymn suits all the believers who are at the bottom of Mount Sion, and begin to join the spirits of just men made perfect. But when the triumphal chariot of perfect love gloriously carries you to the top of perfection's hill; when you are raised far above the common heights of the perfect; when you are almost translated into glory like Elijah, then you may sing another hymn of the same Christian poet, with the Rev. Mr. Madan, and the numerous body of imperfectionists who use his collection of Psalms, etc.

" Who in Jesus confide,
  They are bold to outride
The storms of affliction beneath ;
  With the prophet they soar
  To that heavenly shore,
And outfly all the arrows of death.

>   By faith we are come
>   To our permanent home;
>   By hope we the rapture improve;
>   By love we still rise,
>   And look down on the skies;
>   For the heaven of heavens is love!
>
>   Who on earth can conceive
>   How happy we live
>   In the city of God the great King;
>   What a concert of praise,
>   When our Jesus's grace
>   The whole heavenly company sing!
>
>   What a rapturous song,
>   When the glorified throng
>   In the spirit of harmony join!
>   Join all the glad choirs,
>   Hearts, voices, and lyres,
>   And the burden is 'Mercy divine'!"

But when you cannot follow Mr. Madan, and the imperfectionists of the Lock Chapel, to those rapturous heights of perfection, you need not give up your shield. You may still rank among the perfect, if you can heartily join in this version of Psalm cxxxi.—

>   "Lord, Thou dost the grace impart,
>   Poor in spirit, meek in heart,
>   I will as my Master be,
>   Rooted in humility.
>
>   Now, dear Lord, that Thee I know,
>   Nothing will I seek below,
>   Aim at nothing great or high,
>   Lowly both in heart and eye.
>
>   Simple, teachable, and mild,
>   Awed into a little child,
>   Quiet now without my food,
>   Wean'd from every creature good,

> Hangs my new-born soul on Thee,
> Kept from all idolatry;
> Nothing wants beneath, above,
> Resting in Thy perfect love."

That your earthen vessels may be filled with this love till they break, and you enjoy the Divine Object of your faith without an interposing vest of gross flesh and blood, is the wish of one who sincerely praises God on your account, and ardently prays—

> " Make up Thy jewels, Lord, and show
> The glorious, spotless Church below;
> The fellowship of saints make known;
> And, O my God, might I be one!
>
> O might my lot be cast with these,
> The least of Jesu's witnesses!
> O that my Lord would count me meet
> To wash His dear disciples' feet!
>
> To wait upon His saints below,
> On gospel errands for them go;
> Enjoy the grace to angels given,
> And serve the royal heirs of heaven."

www.ingramcontent.com/pod-product-compliance
Lightning Source LLC
Chambersburg PA
CBHW032115230426
43672CB00009B/1747